Civil War Monuments of Connecticut

Second Edition

To Ross –
Happy Exploring!
Dave Pel

By Dave Pelland

Editor, CTMonuments.net

ISBN: 0984836616
ISBN-13: 978-0-9848366-1-1

DEDICATION

To my family and friends.

Thanks for the support and encouragement, and for driving out of the way and waiting patiently alongside Connecticut's Civil War monuments.

This second edition adds a number of Civil War monuments that have been dedicated in Connecticut since the first edition was published in 2011. It also corrects a few typos that snuck into the first edition (hopefully without introducing new ones).

.

ACKNOWLEDGMENTS

We'd like to thank David Ransom and the Connecticut Historical Society for their helpful compilation, in the early 1990s, of the state's Civil War monuments. Their efforts provided an excellent starting point and background information for our efforts.

We'd also like to thank and congratulate the volunteers who continue to dedicate new Civil War monuments throughout Connecticut, or to refurbish and rededicate existing memorials.

CONTENTS

FAIRFIELD COUNTY

Soldiers' and Sailors' Monument, Greenwich

The Greenwich Soldiers' and Sailors' Monument, dedicated in

1890, stands near the intersection of East Putnam Avenue (Route 1) and Maple Avenue.

The monument is topped by a standard-bearer, a common alternative to the traditional infantryman used in many Civil War monuments. In a pose typical of Civil War monuments featuring standard-bearers, the soldier stands with the flag cradled in his left arm. His right hand rests on the hilt of the sword, ready to draw it out to defend the flag.

The Greenwich monument faces south, and an inscription just above the base lists the town name and a dedication "to her loyal sons who fought for the Union," as well as the years of the Civil War. The front of the monument also lists three battle sites: Kingston (Georgia.), Morris Island (S.C.) and Antietam.

The south face also features decorative elements including a large eagle and a detailed trophy depicting a soldier's cap, bayonet and equipment belt.

The east side of the monument lists Appomattox, Gettysburg, Vicksburg and Port Hudson (La.). The north side lists Drury's Bluff, Petersburg and Deep Run (all in Virginia). The west side lists New-Berne (N.C.), Darbytown Road (Va.), Fort Fisher (N.C.) and Fort Gregg (S.C.).

The monument, which stands on the site of a building used for Civil War recruiting, was supplied by the Lazzari & Barton foundry in Woodlawn, N.Y.

Nearby Monuments

Across Maple Avenue, a plaque on the Second Congregational Church commemorates a 1789 visit by George Washington, who "paused here on the Post Road near this church and afterward wrote in his diary 'the superb landscape which is to be seen from the meeting house is a rich regalia.'" The plaque was dedicated in 1932 during bicentennial celebrations of Washington's birth.

A short walk downhill from the Soldiers' Monument, a 1935 monument erected by the Daughters of the American Colonists honors the first English settlers of Greenwich.

The monument features a bronze plaque attached to the southern face of a boulder. The plaque bears a dedication reading, "In memory of the courageous men who founded the first settlement of the Town of Greenwich in the Connecticut Colony, July 18, 1640."

The monument also includes two lists of names reflecting the assembly of Greenwich from Native Americans land purchases.

About three-tenths of a mile east of the Soldiers' and Founders monuments, Greenwich honors the escape of Gen. Israel Putnam from British forces during the American Revolution. The monument stands at the top of a steep hill, near the corner of East Putnam Avenue and Old Church Road, down which Putnam reportedly rode as British forces invaded Greenwich.

The monument bears a plaque on its west face reading, "This marks the spot where on February 26, 1779, Gen. Israel Putnam, cut off from his soldiers cut off from his soldiers and pursued by British Cavalry, galloped down this rocky steep and escaped, daring to lead where not one of many hundred foes dared to follow."

About a mile south of the Civil War monument, a collection of memorials on Greenwich Avenue honor the town's war veterans. World War II, Korea and Vietnam veterans are memorialized in a small park in front of the Board of Education offices. A statue of World War I aviation pioneer Raynal C. Bolling, who was killed in the war, is nearby. An obelisk honoring World War I veterans and battles stands in front of the Greenwich Post Office.

Soldiers' and Sailors' Monument, Stamford

The city of Stamford honors veterans from the Colonial Wars through World War I with a 1920 monument in the heart of downtown.

The Soldiers' and Sailors' Monument, in St. John's Memorial Park, lists more than 4,400 residents on bronze plaques.

The monument bears the dedication, "In everlasting memory of Stamford's patriots 1641-1918." A peaked roof is topped by a sculpture of three eagles.

The marble monument is based on an ancient Greek memorial honoring Lysicrates that also served as inspiration for the 1904 Soldiers' Monument in Seymour. The Stamford monument features nine columns, and the spaces between the columns honor significant battles in the nation's wars.

The two sections honoring Civil War veterans list the battles of Fort Sumter, Bull Run, Antietam, Fredericksburg, Gettysburg, Chickamauga, the Wilderness, Atlanta, Hampton Roads, Chattanooga, Shenandoah and Appomattox.

The base of the monument features five large plaques listing the names of residents who served in the nation's wars. World War I has two plaques of its own, and shares a plaque with the Spanish-American War and the Civil War. A fourth plaque honors veterans of the Civil War, the Mexican War in the 1840s and the War of 1812, and the fifth lists residents who served in the American Revolution as well as the Colonial and Indian Wars between 1689 and 1763.

The World War I plaques list 26 columns of names, and honor 31 residents killed in the conflict.

The monument, designed by architect George A. Freeman, underwent an extensive cleaning in 2009.

Nearby Monuments

A Doughboy statue with a fountain in its base stands near the southeast corner of the small park, which also features benches and walkways emanating from the Soldiers' and Sailors' Monument.

A 1977 monument near the intersection of Main and Atlantic streets honors those lost in World War II, Korea and Vietnam.

Veterans' Memorial Flagpole, Darien

A four-sided sculpture at the base of a flagpole in the center of the Veterans' Cemetery in Darien honors 2,184 veterans from Connecticut and several other states.

Many of the veterans buried in the cemetery, next to Spring Grove Cemetery on Heckler Avenue, lived at the nearby Fitch Home for Veterans and Their Orphans. The Fitch Home was the first such facility for veterans when it opened in 1864.

The flagpole monument, dedicated in 1936, features four figures representing veterans from the Civil War, the Spanish-American War and World War I. On the west face of the monument, a Civil War soldier is standing with his right arm supported by a rifle. On the east face, a sailor represents veterans of the Spanish-American War. On the south face, a stylized Doughboy figure is standing with his right arm held above his head.

The sculptor, Karl Lang, was a local resident who also created the Timothy Ahern monument in New Haven. Lang also contributed to the carvings at Mount Rushmore.

The flagpole, in a small traffic island, is surrounded by evergreen bushes. The flagpole marks the center of 11 rows of headstones that radiate in eight sections.

In July of 2012, a monument honoring the Gettysburg Address was erected near the flagpole. In addition to the text of the address, a bronze plaque provides historical context about the speech and explains how Lincoln's words continue to honor the heroes buried in national cemeteries.

The Fitch Home for Veterans and Their Orphans was founded in 1864 by Benjamin Fitch, a Darien native and dry goods magnate who was one of the nation's first millionaires by the start of the Civil War. Fitch helped to organize a regiment, and promised to care for any veterans who were wounded in action. In 1864, Fitch donated five acres and built a hospital, chapel, library, residence hall and administrative buildings. A year later, the facility expanded to house children who were orphaned by the war.

In 1888, the facility was taken over by the state. The veterans' home expanded a number of times between then and 1940, when the state opened a new facility for veterans in Rocky Hill.

The former chapel building was moved across Norton Avenue in 1950, and is used today by the local VFW post as well as for community and social events. The cemetery was closed to new veteran internments in 1964.

Soldiers' and Sailors' Monument,
South Norwalk

The Soldiers' and Sailors' Monument in South Norwalk stands in a small park near the intersection of West Washington Street and Martin Luther King Drive.

The granite monument, dedicated in 1900, depicts a caped

infantry soldier, facing southeast, who is holding the barrel of a rifle. He stands atop a round column engraved with a dedication reading, "Erected by the Grand Army of the Republic and the citizens of South Norwalk in memory of her loyal sons 1861-1865."

The back of the column is stamped with the dedication date of October 20, 1900. The monument sits on a four-sided base, with each face bearing the symbol for a Civil War specialty: infantry, cavalry, artillery and the navy.

The monument was ordered from the Smith Granite Company of Westerly, R.I., a prominent supplier of Civil War memorials. A copper box in the monument has a list naming schoolchildren who contributed to the monument's fundraising effort.

Soldiers' Monument, Norwalk

Norwalk honors its Civil War veterans with a monument in Riverside Cemetery.

The Soldiers' Monument, dedicated in 1889, features a granite base in a plot reserved for local veterans. A dedication on the monument's east face reads, "In honor of our dead comrades who fought to save the Union in the War of 1861-1865. Erected by

Buckingham Post No. 12, Dept. of Conn., G.A.R (Grand Army of the Republic), 1889."

The monument is surrounded by 32 graves of Civil War veterans who served in regiments from states including Connecticut, New York, New Jersey and Pennsylvania.

The monument was originally topped by a zinc figure depicting a Civil War soldier. The figure was removed in 2002 after vandalism that included the theft of the soldier's rifle.

The Norwalk Historical Society is raising funds to restore the figure and return it to Riverside Cemetery.

Nine veterans of the Spanish-American War are buried not far from the Civil War plot, and other nearby plots are dedicated to veterans of later wars.

Norwalk's use of a zinc soldier atop a granite base was unique in Connecticut. Stratford dedicated an all-zinc Civil War monument in 1889 that, like the Riverside Cemetery monument, has suffered from deterioration over the years because zinc turns brittle in cold weather. Large-scale white bronze monuments often have difficulty supporting their own weight.

The Civil War monuments in White Plains, New York, and Orleans, Massachusetts, feature zinc soldiers atop granite bases.

Memorial Gun, Rowayton

The Rowayton section of Norwalk honors local veterans with a Civil War cannon mounted at the intersection of Rowayton and Wilson avenues.

The memorial gun, a 100-pounder Parrott rifle, was dedicated in 1901 to honor local Civil War veterans.

A dedication engraved on the front (north) face of the monument's base reads, "Memorial gun. Reminding us of the heroic deeds of our soldiers and sailors of the Republic in the War of the Rebellion for the preservation of the Union. Erected 1901. From USS *Tallapoosa*."

The monument's west face bears a plaque honoring local World War I veterans. The bronze plaque lists 15 names, and honors one local resident who died in the conflict.

The east face of the monuments base bears a plaque honoring local World War II veterans. The plaque lists about 176 names, and highlights one resident killed during the war.

The cannon was made in 1864 at the West Point Foundry in Cold Spring, New York. It was used on the USS *Tallapoosa*, a gunship built at the Boston Navy Yard in 1864. The *Tallapoosa* helped maintain the blockade of Confederate ports during the way, and was used for transport and training after the war.

Wayside Cross, New Canaan

New Canaan honors its war heroes with a large Celtic cross on an historic green.

The Wayside Cross, at the intersection of Main and Park streets, stands on a corner of the triangular green, surrounded by three churches, known as "God's Acre."

The Wayside Cross, dedicated in 1923, features allegorical scenes representing the American Revolution, War of 1812, Civil War, Spanish-American War and World War I.

A dedication on the monument's front face reads, "Dedicated to the glory of Almighty God in memory of the New Canaan men and women who, by their unselfish patriotism, have advanced the American ideals of liberty and the brotherhood of man."

The other sides of the monument's base are inscribed with "service," "sacrifice" and "loyalty."

A 1981 plaque mounted in front of the monument's base lists 36 honored dead from World War II, as well as six residents who died while serving in Vietnam.

Veterans Memorial Green, Wilton

Wilton honors its veterans with a group of monuments in a plaza dedicated in 2010.

The Veterans Memorial Green, at the intersection of Center Street and Old Ridgefield Road, features granite columns of honors and benches. The site is dedicated to honor, "Wilton's fallen heroes who made the supreme sacrifice in America's wars."

The collection of monuments includes six pillars inscribed with the names of local war heroes. The pillar honoring the French and Indian War, fought between 1754 and 1763, lists 10 residents.

The American Revolution column honors 20 residents.

The Civil War has the largest grouping of names, with 34 residents being honored.

The World Wars and Korea share a pillar, with the World War I section listing two names; the World War II section listing 10, and the Korea section listing one.

The Vietnam and Iraq wars also share a pillar, with the Vietnam section honoring eight residents and the Iraq section listing one.

Nearby Monuments

Wilton veterans are further honored with a monument a short

distance south of the Memorial Green site. The memorial, dedicated in 1988, honors all veterans who served in the conflicts between the American Revolution and the Vietnam War.

Heroes of the World Wars are also honored with a monument in Hillside Cemetery, about a half-mile northwest of the Memorial Green. A marker bears a dedication reading, "In memory of those who gave their lives [in] World Wars I and II," above 10 names.

Soldiers' Monument, Danbury

The Soldiers' Monument at West Street and Main Street in Danbury was dedicated in 1880 to honor local Civil War heroes.

The monument, patterned after Hadrian's column in Rome, combines a granite column with a marble standard-bearer. The highlighted battles are listed in a spiral pattern that scrolls up to the decorative details beneath the standard-bearer's platform.

The monument's front (east) base bears a dedication reading, "To our brothers, beloved, honored, revered, who died that our country might live." The west face reads, "The defenders of the Union."

On the column, the monument lists the following battles: Bull Run (near Manassas, Va.), Wilderness (near Spotsylvania, Va.), Antietam, Fredericksburg (Va.), Gettysburg, Chancellorsville (Va.), Petersburg (Va.) and Port Hudson (La.).

The monument, supplied by the Ohio firm of Carpenter & Raymond, sits in a triangular park that also features a flagpole, a decorative lamppost and tasteful shrubbery along its West Street sides.

Unknown and African-American Soldier Monuments, Danbury

The Monument to Soldiers in Unknown Graves, in Danbury's Wooster Cemetery, was dedicated in 1894 to honor Connecticut Civil War veterans who were reported missing after battles. The monument is topped by a granite soldier that, unique among the state's Civil War monuments, is holding a rifle at funeral rest position. Also uncommon is the cross on the monument's south face. (The Connecticut Soldiers' Monument in St. Bernard's Cemetery in New

Haven also displays a cross.)

The west (front) and east sides of the monument are inscribed with the names and unit affiliations of local veterans who were lost in the Civil War.

A bronze plaque has been affixed to the east face of the monument honoring Nathan E. Hickok, a Danbury native who was awarded a Congressional Medal of Honor for capturing a battle flag in 1864 during fighting near Richmond.

Next to the Monument to Soldiers in Unknown Graves is a polished granite monument that was dedicated in 2007 to honor African American veterans who volunteered for Civil War service. The west face of the monument bears a dedication, "to the memory of the black soldiers of Greater Danbury who served in the 29th and 30th Regiments Conn. Volunteer Infantry during the Civil War 1981-1865." The west face also bears an inscribed Grand Army of the Republic medallion.

The east face of the monument bears 70 names from the 29th Conn., and honors 16 who were killed in service, as well as nine names from the 30th Conn., including three who were killed. The monument also lists a dozen names from other Connecticut and New

York regiments and the U.S. Navy, including one soldier who lost his life.

Both monuments are not far from a brownstone obelisk honoring American Revolution General David Wooster, a Stratford native killed by British troops in 1777 during fighting in nearby Ridgefield.

The 29th Regiment Conn. Volunteer Infantry is also honored with a 2008 monument in New Haven's Criscuolo Park.

Soldiers and Sailors Memorial, Danbury

Danbury honors veterans of several wars with a 1931 monument on the West Street green.

The Soldiers and Sailors Memorial, near the intersection of West and Division streets, is dedicated to soldiers and sailors who served in the American Revolution, the Civil War, the Spanish-American War, and World War I.

The monument features a bronze group of four soldiers and a sailor standing atop a round granite pillar. A dedication at the monument's base reads, "Dedicated to the soldiers and sailors of Danbury," along with years in which the various conflicts started (1776, 1861, 1898, and 1917).

The American Revolution and World War I figures are standing, the Civil War figure and sailor are in kneeling positions, and the Spanish-American war figure is crouched with a rifle at the ready. All of the figures have a variety of personal equipment.

The figures were created by sculptor Donald E. Curran, a Darien resident who won a design competition.

To the east of the memorial, a granite boulder bears a plaque, dedicated in 1952, that honors Danbury's World War II veterans.

At the eastern end of the green, a memorial honors president James A. Garfield, a Civil War veteran. The monument was erected in a park on West Wooster Street in 1884 by local philanthropist Edward A. Houseman, and moved to the West Street Green in 1931.

The monument was restored in 1993 after it was struck by a car.

Veterans' Memorial, New Fairfield

New Fairfield honors its war veterans with a monument on the town green.

The New Fairfield Veterans' Memorial, located on Pembroke

Road (Route 37) just north of the intersection with Brush Hill Road (Route 39), was dedicated on September 20, 1997.

The monument features two granite tablets, a flagpole and a dozen markers listing the country's major wars.

The east tablet bears a dedication reading, "To those who fought and served to preserve our freedom, this plaque is dedicated to your brave and courageous acts."

The west tablet honors New Fairfield residents who died in wars, starting with two militia members killed during the French and Indian War.

Nine residents are listed for the Civil War; one for World War I; three for World War II; two for Korea; and three for Vietnam.

The green also features a ship's anchor and a number of benches inscribed with the United States seal.

War Memorial, Ridgefield

A large rectangular monument on Main Street in Ridgefield honors local residents who served in wars between the American Revolution and World War I.

The monument, in front of the Methodist Church on Main Street, was dedicated in 1925. The front (east) face of the monument bears the dedication, "To the memory of the citizens of Ridgefield who served their country in the wars of the Republic 1775-1918. Erected by the people of Ridgefield MCMXXIV (1924)."

The east plaque, along with the dedication, bears ornate decorative details that include cannons, flags, medals, a propeller, a scale and a variety of other symbols.

The north plaque honors 185 Civil War veterans.

The west side of the monument honors veterans of the War of the Revolution (listing nearly 250 names), War of 1812 (five names) and Mexican War (two names).

The south side bears a plaque listing two names of Spanish-American War veterans as well as nearly 150 names of World War I veterans.

Soldiers' and Sailors' Monument, Bethel

Bethel honors 14 Civil War heroes with a granite monument at the top of a hill in Center Cemetery.

The monument, dedicated in 1892, was carved from a 14-foot block of granite and features distinctive decorations. A dedication on the front (north) face reads, "In memory of the soldiers and sailors of Bethel who gave their lives in defence of the Union 1861-1865."

The dedication's carving resembles a scroll that hangs from an eagle near the top of the monument's face. A ribbon unfurled next to the eagle reads "Union," and "Liberty."

The monument's base features an intricately carved trophy featuring two rifles and crossed swords along with a soldier's equipment belt, hat, rucksack and bedroll.

The monument's south face lists the names and regimental affiliations of 14 residents who were killed in the war.

The sides of the monument are mostly rough rock face, other than two granite cannonball pyramids.

The monument was supplied by Miller & Luce of Massachusetts.

Liberty and Peace Monument, Newtown

A tall monument topped by an allegorical standard-bearer honors Newtown's soldiers and sailors.

The monument features three pillars rising from a base that includes stone benches. A dedication on the west face of the monument's base reads, "Newtown remembers with grateful prayers and solemn vows her sacred dead [and] her honored living who ventured all unto death that we might live a republic with independence, a nation with union forever, a world with righteousness and peace for all."

The monument is surrounded by a series of Honor Roll plaques listing local residents who have served in the nation's wars. The front of the monument features a plaque honoring veterans of the Civil War and the World War. Another plaque lists veterans of the American Revolution, the War of 1812, the Mexican War (in the 1840s), the Spanish-American War, and the Mexican Border War (in 1915-16).

Moving counter-clockwise around the base of the monument, plaques list veterans of the Persian Gulf War (1990-91), Vietnam, Korea and World War II.

The helmeted allegorical figure representing Peace stands with a flag, a laurel branch and a chain tucked in her arms.

The monument was designed by Franklin L. Naylor, who was also responsible for a war memorial in Jersey City, N.J.

The monument was erected in 1931 on the site of a former schoolhouse that was later moved and turned into a private home. The monument's formal dedication took place in 1939.

The monument is more commonly known locally as the Soldiers' and Sailors' Monument, but according to the Newtown Historical Society, the artist's original blueprints list the name as the Liberty and Peace Monument.

Soldiers' and Sailors' Monument, Bridgeport

Bridgeport honors local men who served in the Civil War with an elaborate monument in Seaside Park.

The monument features a large granite base with several decorative elements that narrows into a shaft topped by a bronze allegorical figure representing the United States. The monument's side feature bronze statues depicting an infantry soldier and a sailor.

A plaque on the front (southeast) face reads, "Dedicated to the memory of the heroic men of Bridgeport who fell in the late war for the preservation of the Union. July 1876." The plaque also features the conclusion of the Gettysburg Address.

Plaques on the other faces list approximately 180 local residents killed in the war, along with their unit, as well as their date and place of death.

The plaques are aluminum replacements added in 2006 as part of a restoration project initiated by the Friends of Seaside Park and the city of Bridgeport. In 2010, a replacement for a marble statue representing Liberty was added to the arched niche in the monument's middle section. The original statue was removed in the late 1960s due to deterioration and vandalism.

The bronze figures were created by Melzar Mosman, who was also responsible for monuments in Middletown and Danielson, as well as figures on the monument in New Haven's East Rock Park.

The monument stands on the former training grounds of the 17th Regiment, Connecticut Volunteer Infantry. The popularity of venturing to the coast to watch the troops train helped lead to the creation of Seaside Park after the war.

Nearby Monuments

Seaside Park is home for a number of notable monuments, including statues of P.T. Barnum, Elias Howe and Christopher Columbus. The park also features a Spanish cannon that honors veterans of the Spanish-American War, and a memorial to baseball star Roberto Clemente.

Pro Patria Monument, Bridgeport

A large monument in Bridgeport's Mountain Grove Cemetery honors local Civil War dead buried in distant battlefields.

The Pro Patria ("For One's Country" in Latin) monument was dedicated in 1906 by the local Grand Army of the Republic (GAR) post, with funding from the state. The front (south) face of the monument features a large granite plaque that depicts an infantryman and a sailor standing with bowed heads.

The plaque has five columns listing the names, ranks, regimental affiliations, and dates and places of death of local residents killed in the war and not returned for burial. A dedication along the bottom reads, "In loving memory of those who did not return." A scrolling ribbon along the top of the plaque lists the battles of Fort Sumter (S.C.), Vicksburg, Mobile Bay (Alabama), Antietam, Gettysburg and Appomattox.

The monument was created by Bridgeport sculptor Paul Winters Morris, who also created the Abraham Lincoln bust on New Milford's green.

The monument, topped by a bronze sculpture of a soldier's hat, coat and sword, stands at the front of a GAR plot containing 83 graves of Civil War veterans buried after the war. The corners of the GAR plot are marked by pyramids of cannonballs, which is uncommon in that most cannonballs that were incorporated into Civil War monuments were later removed during World War II scrap metal drives.

Nearby Monuments

Mountain Grove Cemetery is the final resting place of P.T. Barnum, circus performers Charles Stratton (better known as Tom Thumb) and Lavinia Warren, children's author Robert Lawson, and a number of Bridgeport's industrial and political leaders.

War Memorials, Trumbull

Trumbull honors its veterans as well as the colonial governor for which the town is named with monuments in front of Town Hall.

A granite monument on the eastern side of the green in front of Town Hall honors Trumbull's veterans. A dedication on the front (northwest) face reads, "Dedicated to the honor and sacrifice of the men and women of this community who served our country in all wars, Trumbull, 1958."

The southeast face lists Trumbull residents lost in wars dating back to the French and Indian War (one name) and continuing through Vietnam (five names). The American Revolution and World War I sections both list one name. The Civil War section lists 16 names, and the World War II section honors 22 residents. (Trumbull's World War II heroes are also honored with a monument in Beach Memorial Park).

Not far from the war memorial, a boulder monument honors the service of 23 veterans from the Trumbull Center section of town in the First World War (including four from one family, three from another and two from a third family).

On the western side of the green, a 2002 statue honors Jonathan Trumbull, for whom the town was named in 1797. Trumbull, a Lebanon native, served as governor from 1769 to 1784. Trumbull had the distinction of being appointed by the British and later being elected by residents of the newly independent state.

The statue, by sculptor John Janvrin Blair, depicts Trumbull holding a Bible in one hand and the Declaration of Independence in the other.

Soldiers' and Sailors' Monument, Stratford

A 35-foot monument topped by a standard-bearer stands at the highest point of Stratford's Academy Hill.

The Soldiers' and Sailors' Monument, dedicated in 1889, is unique in Connecticut because it was cast from zinc, a material used in cemetery monuments in the late 19th and early 20th centuries and marketed as "white bronze."

A dedication on the front (west) face reads, "Dedicated to the memory of those who fought for liberty and saved the Union."

Below the dedication is a poem whose author is not credited on the monument: "Yet loved ones have fallen, and still where they sleep, a sorrowing nation shall silently weep, and spring's brightest flowers with gratitude strew o'er those who once cherished the red, white and blue."

The west side also lists the names of 21 residents killed in the war whose remains weren't returned to Connecticut, and lists the battles of Gettysburg and Antietam.

The south face has a wooden panel that apparently replaced a decorative zinc panel, and lists the battles of Lookout Mountain (Georgia) and Olustee (Florida).

The east face has a panel reading, "Erected by the Stratford Veteran Association and its friends, October 3rd, 1889. The Union must and shall be preserved." The east face also lists the battles of Chancellorsville and the Wilderness (both in Virginia).

The north face lists the battles of Fredericksburg (Virginia) and Fort Wagner (South Carolina), and features a decorative panel with an eagle, the U.S. shield, flags, a drum and crossed cannon.

The Stratford standard-bearer is uncommon in that the soldier has a sword in his right hand. Most other standard-bearer monuments depict the soldier with his hand on a sheathed sword.

Stratford's monument, like most white bronze cemetery markers, was produced by the Monumental Bronze Company of Bridgeport.

Zinc war monuments are very rare, in part because granite and bronze were more fashionable in the late 19th Century. For example, only one zinc regimental monument (honoring the Fourth Ohio Infantry) was allowed at Gettysburg, where veterans responsible for approving the design and placement of monuments generally didn't like the appearance of white bronze.

In addition, the material has difficulty supporting its weight in large monuments. The Stratford monument has been renovated and reinforced, but remains split at the northwest corner of its base.

Nearby Monuments
Near the Civil War monument is Stratford's Walk of Honor,

dedicated in 2005 to honor veterans of World War II and more recent wars. A large archway dedicated to World War II heroes bears the names of 97 residents lost in the conflict.

A Vietnam memorial bears the names of seven residents lost in the conflict. A Korean War monument bears the names of nine residents, and a separate monument has been dedicated to honor disabled veterans.

The walkway area is lined with bricks dedicated to local veterans.

A tree near the Soldiers' and Sailors' monument was planted on October 27, 1958 to mark the 100th anniversary of Theodore Roosevelt's birth.

NEW HAVEN COUNTY

Soldiers' and Sailors' Monument, Milford

Milford honors its Civil War veterans with the 1888 Soldiers' and Sailors' Monument on the town green.

The front (east) side of the monument's base bears a dedication reading, "A tribute to the bravery of the men who risked their lives that the Nation might live, 1861-1865." The east face also features an elaborate trophy with a eagle in front of two crossed flags as well as the monument's 1888 dedication date. The east face also honors the Battle of Gettysburg.

The north face features an anchor honoring the Navy and lists the Battle of Fort Fisher.

The west face includes an inscription reading, "Erected by George Van Horn Post, No 39, G.A.R, and friends." The west face also features a GAR medal and honors the Battle of Appomattox.

The south face honors the artillery service with two crossed cannons, as well as the Battle of Port Hudson (Louisiana).

Information about the monument's supplier or sculptor was likely lost when Milford's Town Hall burned down in 1915.

The monument's base is surrounded by a large planting bed.

Nearby Monuments

Several monuments on Milford's Green honor the contributions of local veterans and firefighters.

Immediately in front of the Civil War monument is a memorial fountain erected to honor Thomas Ford, one of Milford's founders. The fountain is used today as a planter.

A short distance to the east is a 1954 flagpole honoring Milford residents who lost their lives in World War II, Korea and Vietnam. Its 15-sided base includes 13 stone markers listing the names of 93 local residents killed in those conflicts.

Near the western end of the green, a 1986 monument honors veterans of the Korea and Vietnam wars.

Near the eastern end, Milford's World War II veterans are honored with a monument featuring five statues representing the contributions of local soldiers, seamen, airmen and nurses.

Local firefighters are honored with a memorial near the World War II monument.

Just above the east end of the green is Milford's Memorial Bridge. The bridge and tower were dedicated in 1889 to honor the city's original settlers, whose burial sites were lost over the years, as well as Milford's Native Americans.

The bridge features a tower and 29 stones inscribed with the names of local settlers, as well as an eclectic collection of historic artifacts. The bridge's north and south copings are marked with large pink granite stones inscribed with the name of an original settler, as well as the name of his wife and date of his death.

The front entrance also honors the area's original settlers from the Wepawaug nation with a stylized Native American portrait over the doorway and a representation of the mark by which Ansantawae, the nation's sachem, signed the deed for the purchase of Milford.

Soldiers' Monument, Derby

Derby's Civil War monument, on the Elizabeth Street side of the town green, honors soldiers from Derby and Huntington (a predecessor of today's City of Shelton).

The Derby monument has two dedication dates. The base was dedicated in 1877. Six years later, after additional funds were raised, the base was remodeled and the infantryman statue was added. (As a side benefit, this allowed Derby to have two dedication ceremonies, as well as additional parades and parties.)

The west side of the monument bears a dedication reading, "In memory of the men of Derby and Huntington who fell in the service of their country in the War of the Rebellion, 1861-1865, as defenders of liberty and nationality."

The monument's east side bears a dedication, "Erected by the people of Derby and Huntington, A.D. 1883, in honor of all who fought in the service of their country," along with an except from the Gettysburg Address: "That government of the people, by the people, and for the people should not perish from the earth."

The north and south plaques list about 81 names and regimental affiliations of local residents killed during the conflict.

The south side also features a brief excerpt from the "Bivouac of the Dead" poem by Theodore O'Hara, which appears on plaques and monuments in many National and Confederate cemeteries.

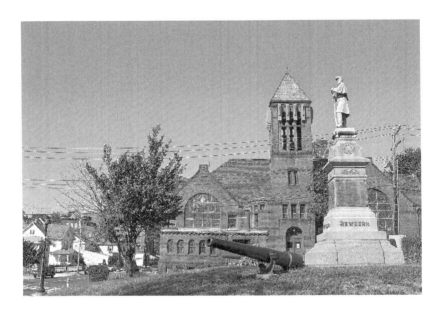

The monument's base has raised inscriptions listing the battles of Atlanta, Chancellorsville (Va.), New Bern (N.C.) and Gettysburg.

The granite section of the monument was supplied by M.J. Walsh, and the bronze figure came from the New York foundry owned by Maurice J. Power. Walsh and Power also collaborated on the Soldiers' Monument in Ansonia's Pine Grove Cemetery.

The four cannons at the base of the Derby monument are 30-pounder Parrott rifles manufactured in 1861 at the West Point Foundry in Cold Spring, New York.

Nearby Monuments

The Derby Green also features monuments to local veterans of the World Wars, Korea and Vietnam, as well as a second memorial listing nine residents who were killed in Korea and Vietnam. A bell at the southwest corner of the green honors local firefighters.

Soldiers' Monument, Ansonia

An 1876 monument in Ansonia's Pine Grove Cemetery honors the service of local heroes killed in the Civil War.

The monument features a statue of an artillery officer standing atop a granite base. A dedication on the rear (south) side of the monument reads, "Ansonia's tribute to the memory of her sons who gave their lives to their country in the rebellion of 1861-1865."

The base of the south side also lists the battle of Antietam. The north side lists the battle of Malvern Hill (Va.). The east side lists the battle of Mobile (Ala.), and Gettysburg is listed on the west side of the monument's base.

The monument's dedication appears on its rear face because the statue has been reversed. When the monument was originally dedicated, it faced south toward the main cemetery entrance on Grove Street. The entrance was later moved to the north (Church Street) side of the cemetery, and the statue was turned around.

The monument is surrounded by four 30-pounder Parrott rifle cannons that were manufactured in 1861. The southwest cannon was mounted upside-down in its bracket, judging from the date and foundry markings on its side. Since the cannon weighs 2.1 tons, we doubt anyone's going to remount it.

The Ansonia monument was designed by sculptor M.J. Walsh of the Maurice J. Power foundry, who also created the Soldiers' Monument on the nearby Derby Green.

Soldiers' Monument, Seymour

A 1904 granite monument in Seymour's French Memorial Park honors the town's Civil War heroes.

The Soldiers' Monument, whose design is based on an ancient Greek monument honoring Lysicrates that also inspired a monument in Stamford, features a granite infantry soldier standing atop a domed shaft supported by six pillars.

A dedication on the front (south) face reads, "This monument is erected by the citizens of Seymour in honored memory of the defenders of our country 1861-1865." Above the open area created by the column, a band lists the battles of Gettysburg, James Island (near Charleston, S.C.), Atlanta and Antietam.

The monument site has changed several times over the years. The round fence, for instance, was added later. The monument also featured a tripod formed by three rifles in the area enclosed by the pillars. The rifles now belong to the Seymour Historical Society after being stolen from the monument and recovered. In addition, a cannonball pyramid has been removed from the site.

The monument also has three 30-pounder Parrott rifles at the base, similar to those found at nearby Civil War monuments in Derby and Ansonia. The markings on the Seymour cannon are difficult to discern, but at least one was forged in 1864 by the West Point Foundry in Cold Spring, N.Y.

The Soldiers' Monument was rededicated in 2011.

Nearby Monuments

A collection of other war monuments stands to the east of the Soldiers' Monument. Residents who served in the two World Wars are honored by a large monument with four plaques (three of which are dedicated to World War II). The World War I plaque lists four columns of residents who served in the conflict, and honors 13 residents who were killed. Each of the three World War II plaques has four columns of names and collectively honor 31 residents who were killed.

A Vietnam monument has four columns of names and honors two residents who were killed. A Korean War monument has three columns and also honors two residents who were killed. A Revolutionary War monument has two columns of names.

Soldiers' Monument, Naugatuck

The Soldiers' Monument in Naugatuck was dedicated in 1885 to honor residents who served in the Civil War.

The monument, which sits at the center of the town green, features a granite shaft topped by a caped infantryman resting with a rifle. The front (east) face of the monument lists the battles of Fort Wagner (S.C., near Charleston), the Wilderness (in central Virginia) and Cedar Mountain (Va.). Just above the base is the dedication by the people of Naugatuck, "In memory of her sons who fought to maintain the Union 1861-1865."

The south face doesn't list any battles, but does ask that the "God of nations preserve our country in the bond of peace now established," a message that reflects a broader spirit of reconciliation the country was experiencing during that era.

The west face of the monument lists the battles of Chancellorsville (Va.), Petersburg (Va.) and Antietam, as well as a dedication to "the citizen soldier, fearless in war, industrious in peace."

The north face lists the battles of Malvern Hill (Va.), Gettysburg and Atlanta, and a message reminding us that "the deeds of those who died in defense of the government of the people are immortal."

The monument was designed and supplied by the Ryegate Granite Company of New York.

Nearby Monuments

An impressive monument on the northeast corner of the Naugatuck Green honors local veterans. The monument features a central slab dominated by an eagle, emblems (in stone and bronze) of the armed services and the inscription, "Naugatuck honors the men and women who served their country in time of need." The center column is flanked by four smaller slabs listing military conflicts since World War II, along with the names of local residents who died in those conflicts.

Naugatuck's World War I monument is located a short walk away on Meadow Street, northwest of the Soldiers' Monument. The monument, which was dedicated in 1921, features a large flagpole base that sits in a small park next to Salem School.

The monument was sculpted by Evelyn Beatrice Longman, whose other works include the Spanish-American War memorial in Hartford's Bushnell Park, decorative elements on the Lincoln Memorial in Washington, D.C., a war memorial in Windsor, and a variety of other sculptures.

Near the World War Monument, a flagpole in front of Salem School (which opened in 1893) serves as a monument to the Spanish-

American War in 1898. A plaque at the base of the flagpole commemorates the USS Maine, which sunk in Havana's harbor after an explosion. Identical plaques adorn memorials in Bridgeport, Meriden and Norwich.

Soldiers' Monument, Prospect

Prospect honors its veterans with a monument in a small park just off Prospect Road (Route 68).

The Soldier's Monument, dedicated in 1907, features an infantryman standing atop a granite base decorated with bronze plaques and a Grand Army of the Republic medal.

A dedication plaque on the monument's front (west) face reads, "To the loyal sons of Prospect who served in the wars of our country. The noblest motive is the public good."

The base of the west face also features a small monument, dedicated in 1977, that honors veterans of World War II, Korea and Vietnam.

The monument's south face has a plaque honoring the 25

Prospect residents who served in World War I. The undated plaque replaced a decorative trophy depicting two crossed rifles.

The east face lists 22 names of residents who fought in the American Revolution and other wars, as well as Prospect's 69 Civil War veterans.

The north face bears the emblem of the Grand Army of the Republic, the post-Civil War veterans' organization.

Perhaps because of its relatively late construction in 1906, the Prospect monument features a number of design elements not commonly seen on other Civil War monuments in Connecticut. For instance, the infantryman's rifle (a model 1861 Springfield musket) was fabricated from bronze. This use of a different material for the soldier and his rifle is unique in Connecticut.

Also unusual is the placement of the soldier's left foot on a rock, as well as the uniform pants being tucked into his footwear. While the practice of tucking in pant legs to guard against ticks was common during the Civil War, this is the only time we've seen it depicted on a monument.

The monument was fabricated by the Thomas F. Jackson Co., which also supplied the Kenea Soldiers' monument in Wolcott.

Not far from the Civil War monument, a small 1897 monument honors the location of the town's original burying ground.

Soldiers' Monument, Waterbury

The elaborate Civil War monument at the west end of Waterbury's green was dedicated in 1884 to honor local residents who served in the conflict, and, uncommonly among monuments of the era, also addresses social changes brought about by the war.

The monument, nearly 50 feet tall, is topped by an allegorical statue representing Victory. She stands atop a granite column that features four bronze statues representing the fact that people from all walks of life participated in (or were affected by) the war.

The west face, for instance, features a farmer clutching a rifle. On the north side, a seated soldier is resting with his bedroll and rifle handy. The east face features a laborer with a sword in his hand.

The sculpture on the south face makes a rare reference to the emancipation of slaves by depicting a woman with a book reading to two children — one is white, and the other is African American. The figures represent the new educational opportunities possible since the elimination of slavery.

The west face also features a bas-relief sculpture depicting a pitched battle, and the east face displays the naval battle between the ironclad ships the *Monitor* and the *Merrimac*.

The south face carries a dedication reading, "In honor of the patriotism and to perpetuate the memory of the more than 900 brave men who went forth from this town to fight in the war for the Union. This monument has been erected by their townsmen that all who come after them may be mindful of their deeds, and fail not in the day of trial to emulate their example."

The north face bears a somewhat florid poem written by the Rev. Dr. Joseph Anderson.

The traffic island hosting the monument features four lampposts with shafts that are shaped like cannons with rifles leaning against them.

Nearby Monuments

A 1958 granite memorial to veterans of all wars stands at the center of Waterbury's green. The monument features a multi-faceted base from which four columns rise. The columns are connected by granite blocks with engraved emblems of the service branches.

Near the War Memorial is a Freedom Tree flanked by two sets of monuments in honor of service members who were declared missing in action during in Korea and Vietnam. The Korea monument has four names, and the Vietnam monument has two.

Kenea Soldiers' Monument, Wolcott

Wolcott honors veterans of the American Revolution, War of 1812 and the Civil War with a monument in the center of town.

The Kenea Soldier's Monument, dedicated in 1916, features an infantry soldier standing atop a relatively simple granite monument. A dedication on the monument's north face reads, "Presented to the town of Wolcott by Leverett Dwight Kenea in memory of the soldiers who fought in the War of the Revolution, the War of 1812 and the Civil War. A.D. 1916."

The soldier stands with a rifle in his right hand, an uncommon variation on the two-handed rifle grip usually seen in monuments with infantry figures. Also, the figure's face appears slightly more mature than the figures seen in other monuments.

The monument was donated by Leverett D. Kenea, a Wolcott native who invested in several successful Thomaston businesses and made a number of philanthropic donations.

The town green is also known as Kenea Park, and Kenea Avenue runs between the green and Town Hall.

The monument, supplied by the Thomas F. Jackson Company of

Waterbury (which also produced the Prospect Soldiers' Monument) was unveiled during its dedication ceremony by Wolcott's four surviving Civil War veterans.

At the east end of the green, a granite monument honors veterans of the two World Wars, Korea and Vietnam, as well as recent conflicts in the Persian Gulf. The monument was dedicated in 1982 with support from three civic organizations.

At the western end of the green, a monument honors the service of local veterans in Operation Desert Storm in 1991.

Soldiers' Monument, Cheshire

Cheshire honors its Civil War veterans with an 1866 obelisk that is among the state's earliest monuments to the war.

The Soldiers' Monument stands on the Cheshire Green, in front of the 1827 First Congregational Church, and across the street from Town Hall.

A dedication on the monument's front (east) face reads, "Erected to the memory of those who enlisted from the town of Cheshire in the Civil War, 1861-1865." The east face also lists 27 names.

The monument's other faces also bear bronze plaques, each listing 33 names of local Civil War veterans.

The reference to the "Civil War" on the dedication reflects the facts that the plaques were attached to the monument in 1916. Most late 19th century monuments refer to the conflict as the "War of the Rebellion" or describe preserving the Union. The term "Civil War" was commonly adopted in the early 20th century.

At its 1866 dedication, the monument originally listed 14 names. As veterans died after the war, additional names were incised into the monument. In 1916, the bronze plaques were created and the monument was rededicated.

The base of the monument's north face is inscribed with "Foote," a reference to Admiral Andrew Hull Foote, who commanded Navy forces that helped with the capture of Fort Henry and Fort Donelson in Tennessee, as well as Island No. 10 on the Mississippi River. Foote's grandfather was a pastor of the Congregational Church, and his father served as a U.S. senator and governor of Connecticut. Foote is buried in New Haven's Grove Street Cemetery.

The base of the monument's south face honors Abraham Lincoln with the inscription of his last name.

Cheshire's Civil War monument was dedicated in July of 1866, making only the 1863 Soldiers' Monument in Kensington (the oldest permanent Civil War monument in the country) and the January 1866 Soldiers' Monument in Bristol (and perhaps the undated Civil War monument in Plymouth) as older. Civil War monuments in Northfield and North Branford were dedicated later in 1866.

Nearby Monuments

Across the street from the Soldiers' Monument, a 1990 memorial honors Cheshire's war veterans. The memorial is not far from the town's World War I monument, which lists local veterans in three columns. A separate section highlights six veterans who were killed in the conflict.

Soldiers' Monument, Meriden

A tall granite obelisk topped by an infantry soldier honors the service of Meriden's Civil War heroes.

The monument stands outside City Hall at the intersection of East Main Street (Route 66) and Liberty Street.

A dedication at the base of the front (west) face reads, "To the memory of our fellow citizens who died in defence of the government 1861-1865. Dedicated 1873."

The front face, like the other three, also bears a bronze plaque that honors about 40 residents killed in the war by listing their name, rank, company, regiment, and the place and date of death. The names are arranged by their company affiliation, which in several instances groups soldiers killed in the same battle.

The memorial plaques are uncommon in that the letters are incised into the plaque, instead of being raised. The Soldiers' Monument in Norwich also uses this technique.

The front face of the obelisk also features the U.S. and Connecticut shields, and lists the battles of Antietam and Gettysburg. The south face honors the battles of Vicksburg and Fort Fisher (N.C.); the east lists Atlanta and Appomattox; and the north lists New Berne and Roanoke Island (both in N.C.)

The monument was created by Batterson, Canfield & Co., which supplied many of the state's Civil War monuments.

A 1948 granite marker on the south side of the main stairs to City Hall commemorates an 1860 political speech by Abraham Lincoln. A marker on the north side of the stairs, made from metal salvaged from the USS Maine, honors Spanish-American War veterans (identical plaques are displayed in Naugatuck, Bridgeport, Norwich, and several other Connecticut cities).

City Hall, a 1907 replacement for a building that burned down, stands atop a small hill. The monument site was once surrounded by a fence that, along with four cannons, was donated to a World War II scrap drive. Small pillars decorated with shields stand at the four corners of the monument's base.

Nearby Monuments

Meriden boasts an impressive collection of military monuments along a nearly quarter-mile stretch of Broad Street (Route 5).

The largest of the monuments, near the intersection of Broad Street and East Main Street, is the city's 1930 World War Monument. The monument, by Italian sculptor Aristide Berto Cianfarani, features four figures at the base of a pointed shaft topped by an eagle.

Not far from the monument is Meriden's World War Wall of Honor, which features six large bronze plaques, each with four columns of names.

Also near the World War monument is the city's 1955 World War II Honor Roll, which features two granite panels with three plaques on each side.

Other monuments on Broad Street include the Gold Star monument honoring war heroes, a Marine Corps monument, monuments to veterans of the Spanish-American War, Korea and Vietnam, and a memorial honoring Polish military commander Casmir Pulaski.

Soldiers' Monument, Wallingford

A resting infantry soldier stands atop a circular-shafted monument dedicated in 1902 in Wallingford's Dutton Park.

The granite monument features a variety of shapes and ornamental details in its different sections. The monument's square base, for instance, is topped by an eight-sided band that in turn gives way to a cone-shaped cylinder. The infantry soldier stands atop a round base.

The monument's front (south) face bears the dedication, "Erected by Arthur H. Dutton Post No. 36 G.A.R. and the people of Wallingford to the memory of the brave men who died that their country might live," as well as ornate carved wreathes inscribed with the Civil War years. (Similar wreaths on the monument honor the Army and the Navy.) The south shaft also bears a carved eagle.

The east face lists the battles of Antietam, Gettysburg, Cedar Mountain (Va.) and Morris Island (S.C.).

The north face lists the battles of Atlanta, New Orleans, Port Hudson (La.) and Appomattox (Va).

The west face lists the battles of New Berne (N.C.), Fort Fisher (N.C.), Chancellorsville (Va.) and Petersburg (Va.)

A granite memorial stone placed in front of the monument lists the names and regimental affiliations of 24 Wallingford residents killed in the Civil War. The memorial is not dated, but was clearly added after the larger monument was dedicated.

The cannon at the south end of the park was cast in 1830 at the West Point Foundry in Cold Spring, N.Y.

Nearby Monuments

A triangular planting bed immediately north of the Soldiers' Monument honors local residents who fought in the American Revolution. Plaques mounted in the base of the nearby flagpole honor local veterans' organizations.

A monument at the north end of the park honors residents who served in the Vietnam War.

War Memorials, North Haven

North Haven honors local veterans with a collection of monuments on the green across from its 1886 Memorial Town Hall.

Near the southern end of the green, the town honors Civil War veterans with a 1905 monument that features an 1867 Rodman gun mounted on a stone base. A dedication on the base's front (west) face reads, "Erected by the town of North Haven as a tribute to the valor of her sons who on land and sea fought in the Civil War to preserve the Union."

The east face lists the monument's 1905 dedication date and honors the battles of Cedar Mountain, Fort Wagner, Fredericksburg, Fort Gregg, and Petersburg (all in Virginia).

The cannon was manufactured in 1867 at the Fort Pitt Foundry in Pittsburgh, and was one of four installed at Lighthouse Point in New Haven. Another Lighthouse Point cannon stands as a Civil War monument on the East Haven green. Another that was placed near Milford's Town Hall was lost to a World War II scrap drive.

Nearby Monuments

Also north of the Civil War monument are memorials to local veterans who served in Vietnam and Korea. Those wars are commemorated with Honor Roll plaques mounted on granite monuments.

Moving farther north, we find North Haven's World War II monument, which features two plaques listing local veterans in 10 columns. The right side of the monument also lists seven residents killed in the conflict as well as one who was missing in action. The left side has a plaque honoring nine residents who were held as prisoners of war.

Across Church Street stands North Haven's 1886 Memorial Town Hall, which was the town's first tribute to its Civil War veterans. Just inside the lobby are plaques listing local veterans who served in the Civil War and World War I, and a monument honoring all war veterans stands in front of the building.

The plaque listing residents who served in the Civil War replaced a marble memorial (now owned by the North Haven Historical Society) that listed residents who died in the war.

The erection of a memorial hall and a Civil War monument reflects a debate held in several Connecticut towns whether to honor veterans with a monument or a civic building. As was the case in Madison, monument supporters continued campaigning well after a town hall had been constructed and the municipality eventually erected both.

Soldiers' Monument, North Branford

An 1866 obelisk on the North Branford town green was among the first monuments in the state to honor Civil War veterans.

The monument stands on the green along Foxon Road (Route 80), next to the Congregational Church, and was dedicated in April of 1866 — about a year after the war's conclusion. The monument bears a simple inscription on its front (southeast) face reading "Our Soldiers" and the year 1865.

The northeast face of the monument lists the names, units and places of death of two local soldiers killed in the war. The northwest face lists three residents and the southwest face honors two Civil War heroes.

The monument was supplied by the Westerly, R.I., firm of Burdick & Company, with the lettering performed by the Stony Creek firm of Greene & Turner.

Nearby Monuments

The Civil War monument is one in a series of memorials along the town green. Moving south, the next monument is a boulder with a bronze plaque that honors World War I veterans. The plaque bears the dedication "to the men who served their country during the World War" and lists 17 names.

Next comes another stone memorial with a plaque, apparently of recent vintage, with four columns of names honoring veterans of World War II. A separate monument, further south, honors six local residents who were killed in the war.

Completing the monument collection on the green is a rough boulder at the southern end dedicated to residents who served in the Vietnam War.

War Memorial Boulder, Northford

A boulder on Middletown Avenue in the Northford section of North Branford honors local residents who served in the wars between the American Revolution and World War II.

The boulder was first dedicated in 1920, when the bronze plaque on the front (east) face honored veterans of the American Revolution, Civil War and the World War. The monument's dedication reads "Erected in 1920 by the Society of Northford in honor of her sons who answered their country's call."

The American Revolution section lists 50 names. The Civil War section has 32 names, and the World War Honor Roll lists nine residents who served in the conflict.

The boulder sits in a small triangular green where Middletown Avenue intersects with Clintonville and Old Post roads, near the Northford Congregational Church.

The rear side of the monument bears an undated plaque that honors World War II veterans. The plaque lists the names of 78 local residents who served in the war, with stars indicating the names of two residents who were killed in the conflict.

Soldiers' and Sailors' Monument, New Haven

The 110-foot tall Soldiers' and Sailors' Monument high above New Haven is visible for miles on a clear day.

The monument, at the summit of East Rock Park, was dedicated in 1887 to honor soldiers and sailors who fought in the American

Revolution, the War of 1812, the Mexican-American War and the Civil War.

The monument features a granite column rising from a square base with allegorical bronze statues on the four corners, and bas relief sculptures depicting scenes from the highlighted wars.

The monument is topped by an 11-foot-tall statue, known as the Angel of Peace, that faces downtown New Haven and holds an olive branch in an outstretched left arm. The statue, originally installed in March 1887, was restored in 2006.

Four allegorical statues appear on the corners of the monument's base. The west corner depicts History holding a book, and the south corner symbolizes Patriotism bearing a sword. The east corner represents Victory, and the north corner depicts Prosperity.

The front (southwest) face of the monument honors the Civil War, and lists the battlefields of Gettysburg, Port Hudson (La.) and Fort Fisher (N.C.). A scene on the southwest face depicts Robert E. Lee's surrender of the Army of Northern Virginia at Appomattox Court House, Va. in April of 1865. In this scene, Lee appears to have a painful headache, which, under the circumstances, is probably understandable.

The southwest face also has a door to the interior of the monument, where a staircase leads to an upper-level viewing area that is open to the public periodically.

The monument's southeast face honors the American Revolution by listing the battlefields of Bunker Hill, Bennington (Vermont) and Saratoga (N.Y.) below a scene depicting the British surrender at Yorktown in 1781.

The southeast face also bears one of two large bronze plaques with 520 names of soldiers and sailors from New Haven who died in the Civil War. The plaques, which were added to the monument in 1894, have ornate borders with raised moldings and ribbons that feature regimental emblems and the names of Civil War battlefields.

The northeast (rear) face of the monument honors the War of 1812 by listing battlefields near Lake Erie, Lake Champlain and New Orleans and a hard-to-discern naval scene. The rear face has a doorway that is either false or has been cemented over.

The northwest face honors the 1846 Mexican-American War by listing battlefields including Palo Alto (near Brownsville, Texas), Molino Del Rey and Chapultepec. A scene from that war appears above a second plaque listing local Civil War heroes.

The monument's dedication in June of 1887 was attended by Union generals William Tecumseh Sherman and Philip Henry Sheridan. A parade of 20,000 people was watched by a crowd estimated at more than 100,000.

The ornate bronze plaques listing the Civil War dead were added seven years later.

The monument's surroundings have changed over the years. For instance, a small pavilion that stood at the summit has been removed, as was a cannon placed near the monument. Later, a small plaza and fence were added to the monument's base.

The monument was rededicated during ceremonies held in 2012.

Broadway Civil War Monument, New Haven

A column at the intersection of Elm Street and Broadway in New Haven honors the service of four Connecticut regiments during the Civil War.

The 32-foot column, topped by a bronze eagle and flanked by two granite soldiers, was dedicated on June 16, 1905, to honor three infantry regiments and an artillery regiment.

A dedication on the front (south) face on the monument reads: "Erected by the joint contributions of the State of Connecticut and the Veteran Associations of 1st Conn. Light Battery and 6th, 7th and 10th Conn. Vols. as a sacred and perpetual memorial to men who suffered and died that the Republic might live: 1861-1865."

Beneath this dedication, a bronze plaque honors the 10th Conn. Volunteer Infantry, which participated in 51 engagements between Sept. 1861 and Sept. 1865. Among the 1,879 soldiers who enrolled in the regiment, there were 1,011 casualties. The bottom of the plaque bears the inscription "Safe and happy the republic whose sons gladly die in her defense."

On the east side of the monument, a figure depicts an infantry soldier reaching into an ammunition bag. On the base beneath his feet, a bronze plaque honors the Seventh Connecticut Volunteer Infantry regiment, which participated in battles in South and North Carolina and Georgia, as well as "13 other engagements."

The west side of the monument features a figure depicting an artilleryman scanning the horizon while holding a ramrod in his left hand. A plaque beneath this figure honors the 1st Conn. Light Battery, which served between Oct. 1861 and June 1865. Major engagements cited on the plaque include the siege of Charleston, and the Richmond and Petersburg campaigns in Virginia.

A plaque on the monument's south side commemorates the 6th Conn. Volunteer Infantry, which served between Sept. 1861 and August 1865. The regiment had a total enrollment of 1,608 and suffered 807 casualties during engagements in Virginia, South Carolina and Georgia.

The monument was designed and constructed by the Smith Granite Company of Westerly, R.I.

Just north of the Civil War monument is Christ Church, which was built in 1895. A monument outside the south side of the church is dedicated to George Brinley Morgan, who became pastor of the church in 1878 and was killed in a motor car accident in 1908.

9th Regiment Monument, New Haven

A 1903 granite monument dedicated to a Civil War regiment comprised primarily of Irish Americans stands in New Haven's Bay View Park.

The 9th Regiment Connecticut Volunteers monument is located in a park that served as the unit's training ground and home for a few months following its formation in 1861. A caped infantryman stands with a rifle atop a short granite pillar.

The front (south) face of the monument bears the Connecticut seal above the name of the regiment and "1861-1865". The base of the monument also lists the battle of New Orleans.

A bronze plaque on the east face lists nearly 100 names of unit members who died in service as well as the battle of Baton Rouge. The north face lists 80 names and the battle of Cedar Creek (Va.), and the west face lists 85 names as well as Fishers Hill (Va.)

The monument has undergone several changes since its 1903 dedication. Originally, the monument's decorative elements were painted gold. If you look closely at the monument, traces of the gold paint can be seen (such as in the dash between 1861 and 1865).

In addition, the monument was moved in 1950 from its original location to accommodate the construction of Interstate 95.

Four cannons surrounding the monument were removed from

their carriages and re-mounted on concrete bases. The cannons are original Civil War 12-pounder Dahlgren guns, which were known as "boat howitzers" that could be mounted on carriages and brought ashore for land use.

A monument honoring the 9th Regiment was dedicated in October 2008 at the Vicksburg National Military Park.

29th Regiment Monument, New Haven

Connecticut's African American Civil War veterans are honored with a 2008 monument in New Haven's Crisculo Park.

Descendants of the Connecticut 29th Colored Regiment, Connecticut Volunteer Infantry, have honored the 900 soldiers who fought with the regiment with a black granite monument. Eight smaller monuments, listing members of the regiment, are arranged in an arc ranging from the north to the south. The smaller monuments also list the towns — from Avon to Woodstock — from which members joined.

On the large monument's west face, a bronze bas relief plaque depicts soldiers carrying the United States flag and the unit's colors while others stand by with rifles. Below the plaque, the unit's six engagements are listed.

The west face also lists 45 officers and enlisted men killed or mortally wounded, as well as 152 men who died from disease or accident.

The south face is inscribed with a detailed history of the unit, which rallied on the site of today's Crisculo Park (then known as Grapevine Point) and departed for the war in March of 1864.

The east face has an illustration depicting two soldiers, and the north face lists the 2008 dedication by the regiment's descendants.

The monument was created by sculptor Ed Hamilton, who was also responsible for the Amistad memorial at New Haven's City Hall.

Members of the CT 29th regiment from the greater Danbury area are honored with a 2007 monument in the city's Wooster Cemetery.

Woolsey Hall, New Haven

Yale honors students and graduates killed in the country's wars with memorials in Woolsey Hall.

The concert hall's lobby walls feature large marble slabs, arranged by war, inscribed with the names, military and Yale affiliations, and date and place of death.

The Civil War memorial, flanking the corridor between the hall's rotunda and its west entrance, was dedicated in 1915. Reflecting the spirit of reconciliation common at the time of dedication, the memorial blends Yale graduates and students who died while serving in Union and Confederate forces.

The floor between the memorial plaques has an inset dedication reading, "To the men of Yale who gave their lives in the Civil War. The university has dedicated this memorial that their high devotion may live in all her sons and that the bonds which now unite the land may endure. MCMXV (1915)."

Below the dedication, which is becoming hard to read after years of foot traffic, is evidence of an earlier inscription.

The Civil War tablets list 113 killed defending the Union, and 54 killed serving the Confederate states.

The north wall features allegorical figures representing peace and devotion. Peace is depicted as a woman holding a child and an olive branch, and an inscription above her head reads, "Peace crowns their act of sacrifice." Devotion is pictured as a toga-draped flag-bearer. An inscription reads, "Devotion gives a sanctity to strife."

The south wall features allegorical depictions of Memory and Courage. Memory is depicted as a woman holding an hourglass, and an inscription reads, "Memory here guards their ennobled names." Courage is pictured as a classical warrior, and his inscription reads, "Courage disdains fame and wins it."

Among the students and graduates honored is Uriah Nelson Parmelee, a Guilford native who left Yale as a junior. He served with a New York regiment and was named a captain in the 1st Connecticut Cavalry before he was killed April 1, 1865, at the Battle of Five Forks in Virginia. Parmelee was killed less than two weeks before Lee's surrender at Appomattox.

The memorial also honors Francis Stebbins Bartow, a law school graduate and Georgia native. A fervent secessionist, Bartow organized an infantry company and was killed during the first Battle of Bull Run/Manassas in 1861. Bartow was the first brigade commander killed in the war.

The memorial was created by sculptor Henry Hering, whose other notable works include the World War plaza and memorial at the

American Legion's headquarters in Indianapolis.

Veterans of other wars are honored with similar tablets along the lobby's interior hallway. In 1920, for instance, the university added eight tablets honoring 225 graduates and students killed during World War I.

The west lobby also contains plaques honoring graduates killed while serving as missionaries, including several who died during the Boxer Rebellion in China.

Woolsey Hall, at the corner of Grove and College streets, was dedicated in 1901 as part of the celebration of Yale's bicentennial.

Soldiers' Monument, New Haven

The Soldiers' Monument in New Haven's St. Bernard's Cemetery was dedicated in 1889 by the state of Connecticut to honor residents killed in the Civil War.

The monument depicts a standard-bearer atop a tall granite

monument. As is typical with standard-bearer poses, the soldier stands with the flag cradled in his left arm, and his right hand rests on the hilt of his sword.

A dedication on the front (east) face of the monument's base reads, "Erected by the State of Connecticut in loving and grateful memory of her sons who offered their lives that the Union should not perish 1861-1865."

The east face of the monument's tall shaft displays a cross. The cross is an uncommon design element among the state's war memorials, and probably reflects the monument's construction in a Catholic cemetery.

A stone eagle graces the column, beneath the soldier's feet, and the other three sides display carved depictions of the United States shield.

During the Civil War, Connecticut furnished 55,861 troops, sailors and marines to the Union effort, and 5,354 were killed in battle, or died of disease, as prisoners, in accidents or from other causes.

The area around the base of the monument in St. Bernard's holds the grave sites of numerous veterans not only of the Civil War, but also other conflicts.

The monument was supplied by the Smith Granite Company of Westerly, Rhode Island. The sculptor was Edward Ludwig Albert Pausch, whose other works included monuments at Antietam and Gettysburg, and a statue of George Washington in Pittsburgh.

Knight Hospital Monument, New Haven

The Knight Hospital Monument in New Haven's Evergreen Cemetery was dedicated in 1870 to honor wounded Civil War veterans who died in the hospital while recovering from battlefield wounds.

The front (northeast) face of the monument bears a dedication reading, "Dedicated A.D. 1870 by the State of Connecticut to commemorate the services and perpetuate the memory of the two hundred and four Union soldiers who died in Knight Hospital, in New Haven, in the years 1862, 3, 4 & 5, and were buried in these grounds."

The monument's column, topped by a bearded infantryman, also bears the Connecticut and U.S. emblems and a decorative trophy with crossed flags, cannons and other military symbols.

The northeast face of the monument also lists the battles of several important battles, including Gettysburg and Fort Fisher (N.C). The northwest face honors Antietam and Chickamauga (Georgia), and the southwest face lists Vicksburg (Mississippi) and Malvern Hill (Virginia). The southeast faces lists New Berne (N.C.) and Fredericksburg (Virginia).

The monument was supplied by James Batterson, a Hartford dealer responsible for several Connecticut Civil War monuments.

More than 120 graves of Civil War veterans are located around the base of the monument, which is located on the Winthrop Avenue side of Evergreen Cemetery.

Knight Hospital was a temporary facility that opened in 1862 to treat soldiers wounded in the Civil War. The U.S. government leased a building from New Haven's State Hospital, a predecessor of today's Yale-New Haven Hospital. The hospital was named after Jonathan Knight, president of General Hospital Society of Connecticut's board and a professor at the Medical Institution of Yale College.

Knight Hospital treated more than 25,000 patients during the Civil War, which impressed us considering the difficulty of transporting wounded soldiers from distant battles to Connecticut during the war.

Soldiers' Memorial, Westville

A memorial gateway in the Westville section of New Haven honors local residents who served in the Civil War.

The 1915 monument, at the entrance to the city's Beecher Park, stands at the corner of Whalley Avenue and Philip Street. Two plaques on the front (northeast) face of the monument bear a dedication reading, "Erected by the Westville Soldiers Memorial Association to commemorate those who enlisted from this place in the War of 1861-1865."

The plaque on the left pillar (as you face the monument) lists 32 names, and the plaque on the right pillar lists 33. The left column also bears the seal of the United States, and the right column bears the Connecticut seal.

Benches extend from the monument's pillars, and bronze letters embedded in the walkway between the columns read, "Soldiers' Memorial A.D. 1915."

The monument was constructed from local traprock, most likely from the West Rock formation that stands just west of the park. The gateway was designed by architect Ferdinand Von Beren.

Cornelius S. Bushnell Monument, New Haven

New Haven honors shipping and railroad investor Cornelius Scranton Bushnell, best known for his contributions to Civil War ironclads, with a monument in Monitor Square.

The 1906 monument near the intersection of Chapel Street and Derby Avenue honors Bushnell, a Madison native who operated a marine supply business, served as president of the New Haven and New London Railroad, and opened a Fair Haven shipyard.

During the Civil War, Bushnell's political and naval connections were instrumental in the development of the USS *Monitor*, the first Union ironclad warship. Bushnell was one of three owners of the vessel during its first battle, after which the U.S. government agreed to purchase the ship and use its design for additional ironclads.

The monument's east face bears a bronze portrait of Bushnell and John Ericsson, the Swedish inventor who designed the *Monitor*.

A dedication on the east face reads, "This memorial is erected in honor of Cornelius Scranton Bushnell, a citizen of New Haven to whose faith, persistence and patriotism the country is indebted for the construction of the *Monitor* from plans by John Ericsson. The *Monitor* defeated the *Merrimac* March 9th 1862."

The monument is topped with large eagle standing on a sphere, supported by four fish, and the United States shield.

The monument was produced by sculptor Herbert Adams, whose other works include bronze doors at the Library of Congress, tablets at the Massachusetts State House and a number of other statues.

After the war, Bushnell was an investor and executive with the Union-Pacific railroad. He died in New York in 1896 and is buried in New Haven's Evergreen Cemetery.

Soldiers' and Sailors' Monument, West Haven

The Soldiers' and Sailors' Monument in West Haven's Oak Grove Cemetery sits in a traffic island near the center of the cemetery. Inscriptions on the front (south) face bear the years of the Civil War, along with a dedication reading, "Erected in honor of our loyal soldiers and sailors."

The south face also displays a bronze trophy with an eagle, crossed flags, swords, oak leaves and cannons. The obelisk is topped by a polished granite sphere, and a carved stars-and-stripes motif surrounds the monument's top.

A smaller granite marker at the base of the monument was dedicated in 1964. The inscription reads, "In grateful tribute to the living and the dead who, through their valiant effort and supreme sacrifice, have helped to preserve us a free nation."

The curbing around the monument bears of the names of several Civil War veterans who were originally buried near the monument, but were moved in subsequent years.

The monument, supplied by the Smith Granite Company of Westerly, Rhode Island, was dedicated in 1890. At the time, West Haven was part of Orange.

Soldiers' Memorials, East Haven

A large cannon honoring Civil War and American Revolution

veterans is one of several war memorials on the East Haven green.

The cannon, a Civil War Rodman gun, was dedicated in 1911. A plaque on the western face of its base reads, "This tribute to the worth of her sons, who have by land and sea offered their lives in defense of their country, is erected by the citizens of East Haven."

The western face of the cannon also features a plaque, dedicated in 2002,listing 16 residents who died in the American Revolution.

The eastern face has a similar plaque listing 15 men killed during the Civil War, including two who died in the Confederate prisoner of war camp in Andersonville, Georgia.

The cannon was one of four originally installed at Lighthouse Point in New Haven Harbor. After the Spanish-American War, the cannons were donated to East Haven, North Haven and Milford for use as war memorials. The East Haven and North Haven cannon are both displayed today, but the Milford Rodman gun was later donated to a World War II scrap drive.

Nearby Monuments

The cannon is one of several monuments on East Haven's green. The northwest corner features a 1988 granite pillar, topped with a globe, that is dedicated to all of East Haven's veterans.

Heroes lost in the two World Wars are listed on plaques mounted on pink granite monuments. The World War I plaque lists five names, while the World War II plaque lists 24 names.

A monument in the southwest corner of the green honors the service of local firefighters.

Soldiers' Monument, Branford

Branford honors its Civil War veterans with a 1885 monument on a hilltop between Town Hall and the Congregational Church.

The monument features a standard-bearer standing atop a granite obelisk. A dedication on the front (north) face reads, "Branford. To her brave sons who fought in the War of the Rebellion, 1861-1865. One country, one flag."

The north face also lists the battles of Antietam and Fredericksburg, and bears a Grand Army of the Republic emblem with two crossed rifles.

The west face lists the battles of Shiloh and Gettysburg, and the south face lists Vicksburg and Port Huron, Michigan. The east face lists battles in New Berne, N.C, and Chancellorsville (Va.).

Four United States seals decorate the top of the shaft, just below the standard-bearer's feet. The Branford monument is similar to the monument in New Haven's St. Bernard Cemetery, which was produced by the same stonecutter at the Smith Granite Company in Westerly, Rhode Island.

Nearby Monuments

A World War I monument on the south side of Branford's Town Hall features a large representation of the Distinguished Service Cross medal. The monument, designed by local resident J. Andre Smith, was dedicated in 1923 and restored in 2006.

A granite monument beneath a flagpole in the center of the town green honors residents who were disabled or killed in World War II, Korea and Vietnam. The monument is not dated, but was likely dedicated in the late 1950s or early 1960s.

Soldiers' Monument, Guilford

A two-toned monument of pink and gray granite honoring Civil War veterans stands at the center of the Guilford green.

The monument, featuring an infantryman standing with a rifle, was completed in two stages that were dedicated 10 years apart. The base, made of pink granite quarried locally, was dedicated in 1877. The soldier, made of gray granite and supplied by a Massachusetts firm, was dedicated in 1887.

Such a delay in the construction of Civil War monuments, while not common, was not unique to Guilford. The figure atop the Soldiers' Monument on the Derby Green, for instance, was dedicated six years after the base.

The dedication on the front (south) face of the monument reads, "In memory of the men of Guilford who fell and in honor of those who served in the war for the Union, the grateful town erects this monument, that their example may speak to coming generations." The south face also lists the battle of Antietam, as well as the names and regimental affiliations of 14 residents killed in the war.

The east face lists Gettysburg and an additional 14 names. The north face, which is harder to read, lists Fredericksburg (Va.) and an estimated 15 names. The west face lists Port Royal (S.C.) and 14 names. The first name listed on the west face is Douglas Fowler, a Guilford native who was commanding the 17th Conn. Volunteer Regiment when he was killed on the first day of the Battle of Gettysburg (July 1, 1863).

Nearby Monuments

On the southwest corner of the green, a boulder bears a bronze plaque dedicated "In honor of our men and women who served in the World War 1917-1918." The monument also lists the names of about 97 residents, as well as four names of residents who gave their lives in the conflict.

The town's World War II monument, on the southeast corner of the green, features three blocks of pink granite. The central block, the largest of the three, honors 16 residents who died in the war by listing their names, ranks and service affiliations. The blocks to the east and west bear plaques describing Guilford's contributions to the war, including the fact that 500 men and women served in the military as well as the wartime efforts of local farms and businesses.

The Vietnam war sacrifice of three residents is honored by a 1984 monument on the northwest corner of the green. That granite monument bears the dedication, "Each peaceful dawn in this place we are reminded of these men who died for their country."

A tree near the Vietnam monument has been dedicated to the memory of 9/11 victims, and a monument near the northeast corner of the green honors local firefighters.

Guilford Gun, Guilford

A large cannon in the northeast corner of Guilford's Alderbook Cemetery honors local Civil War veterans.

The cannon, a 100-pounder Parrott rifle manufactured in 1863, was dedicated in 1902 to honor veterans buried nearby. The cannon points southeast, and has been mounted on a stone platform inscribed with the initials G-A-R to honor the Grand Army of the Republic, the Civil War veterans' organization.

A plaque on the southwest face reads, "To the memory of those who fought for the preservation of the Union 1861-1865."

Concrete footings near the cannon indicate where the monument once had two displays of cannonball pyramids, but those have been removed (most likely for a World War II scrap drive).

The Parrott rifle, probably used by the Navy, bears a distinctive band near the breech, and the markings include the initials of the designer, Robert Parker Parrott.

Memorial Town Hall, Madison

Madison honors its war veterans with an 1897 memorial hall at the east edge of the town green.

Marble plaques mounted near the main (southwest) entrance to the building list the names, rank and regimental affiliation of "Madison volunteers in the war for the Union 1861-1865." The two plaques have about 68 names each.

Immediately alongside the entrance, similar marble plaques list residents who served in the First World War. An honor roll inside the building lists the names and dates of death of four residents who died in the American Revolution; 41 who were killed in the Civil War; seven who were killed in World War I; nine in World War II; three in Korea; and three in Vietnam.

The high total for the Civil War reflects in part the concentration of Madison residents in the 14th Regiment of the Connecticut Volunteer Infantry, which saw its first action at the Battle of Antietam less than three months after being formed in May of 1862. Of the 41 Madison residents killed in the Civil War, a dozen died between Antietam (September 17) and the end of 1862.

Memorial Town Hall, as the building is known today, was built to honor the town's Civil War veterans. Like several communities in the state, Madison was divided on the idea of erecting a Civil War monument or using the money for a civic building.

In the end, Madison got both because Vincent Meigs Wilcox a wealthy merchant who had donated to the Memorial hall fundraising efforts, also sponsored the construction of the Wilcox Soldiers' Monument about three-quarters of a mile to the west in Madison's West Cemetery.

Memorial Hall served as a community and recreation center until 1938, when it was converted into Madison's Town Hall. In 1995, when the current town hall was built, the building was renovated again and today hosts several municipal offices and meeting rooms, as well as the Charlotte L. Evarts Memorial Archives.

Nearby Monuments

A bust outside the hall honors James Madison, the fourth president of the United States. A series of nearby monuments honor the service of local veterans in the American Revolution, World War I, and World War II, Korea and Vietnam.

Wilcox Soldiers' Monument, Madison

A privately funded monument in Madison's West Cemetery honors veterans of the Civil War as well as earlier conflicts.

The 1896 monument, featuring a bronze infantry soldier atop a granite base, was sponsored by Vincent Meigs Wilcox, a Madison native who served as a colonel in the 132nd Pennsylvania volunteer infantry regiment.

A dedication on the front (south) face of the monument reads, "To the memory of the soldiers of Madison, presented by Vincent Meigs Wilcox, New York City, Col. 132d Regt. Pa. Vols., born in Madison, Oct. 17, 1828."

The south face also includes a bronze shield with crossed rifles symbolizing infantry units, and the battle of Antietam is inscribed on the monument's shaft.

The east face lists the battle of Fredericksburg on its upper die, and honors eight officers (including Meigs) by name and includes the inscription "and 158 others."

The north face combines the Civil War and the War of 1812 by listing the battle of Chancellorsville, as well as the years 1812-1814. The names of two officers are inscribed, as are "and 32 others."

The west face honors the battle of Gettysburg and the American Revolution. Under the years 1775-1783 are listed the names of three officers, and the inscription "and 65 others."

The monument, sculpted by Henrich Manger, was sponsored by Meigs after debate among Madison's citizens about the proper way to honor its Civil War veterans. Madison decided a memorial hall was a more practical tribute than a monument, so Meigs decided to build a monument.

Meigs grew up in Madison and served in the Connecticut militia in 1856 before moving to Scranton, Penn. He joined the 132nd infantry regiment as a lieutenant colonel, and assumed command of the regiment during the Battle of Antietam when the unit's colonel was killed.

After the war, Meigs was an executive in two New York photography businesses. Unfortunately, he died a few months before the monument's dedication on July 4, 1896.

MIDDLESEX COUNTY

Soldiers' and Sailors' Monument, Clinton

A granite infantry soldier stands atop a Civil War monument on Clinton's Liberty Green.

The monument, dedicated in 1911, features the soldier and a granite base with curved sides that narrow as they rise toward the figure. A bronze plaque on the front (south) face reads, "Erected by the Woman's Relief Corps and the citizens of Clinton in memory of the soldiers and sailors who fought to preserve the Union 1861-1865. For the dead a tribute, for the living a memory, for posterity an emblem of loyalty to the flag of their country."

Other than the plaque, the monument bears no writing. A state of Connecticut seal appears on the monument's north face. The monument is surrounded by a chain supported by four stone pillars, and a cannon used in the War of 1812 stands alongside it.

The monument was supplied by the Fox-Becker Granite Company of Middletown.

The Woman's Relief Corps was an auxiliary of the Grand Army of the Republic, and was also responsible for the Soldiers' Monument in Putnam. The WRC's involvement and the relatively late dedication date may reflect Clinton's women finally taking action after waiting 40 years for the town's male veterans to build a monument.

Nearby Monuments

About three-tenths of a mile west along East Main Street (Route 1), a monument in front of Town Hall honors residents who served in other wars. The central panel on the front (north) face lists 10 residents who were killed in the two World Wars and Korea. The two side panels list those who served in the World Wars, and the three panels on the monument's south face list residents who served in the nation's other conflicts.

War Monument, Durham

A monument near the south end of Durham's green honors local residents who served in United States wars from the American Revolution to the present day.

The north face of the monument bears the dedication, "Durham honors those who served their country." Plaques on the north face honor veterans of World War I, World War II and Korea.

The central plaque on the south face honors service in the American Revolution, the War of 1812 and the War with Mexico. Other plaques on the monument honor the Civil War, Vietnam, Desert Storm/Shield, and the conflicts in Iraq and Afghanistan.

The monument, surrounded by a chain and stone pillars, sits near the base of a flagpole.

Soldiers' Monument, Middletown

Middletown honors its Civil War veterans with several memorials, including the 1874 Soldiers' Monument on the city's South Green.

The monument features a bronze infantry figure atop a granite base. A dedication on the front (northeast) face of the monument reads, "Erected by the Town of Middletown to the memory of her fallen sons 1874." The front also has a bronze plaque depicting a farming family and a scrolling ribbon bearing an additional dedication reading, "Their heroic valor ensured our lasting peace."

A small round plaque below the soldier's feet bears an additional inscription, "Honor to the brave," inside an ornamental wreath.

The northwest, southwest and southeast sides of the monument bear large plaques listing the name, regimental affiliation, and date and place of death of local residents who were killed in action, or who died of wounds, in prison or after the war.

The rear (southwest) side also features a bronze inset with a wreath and the inscription, "We cherish their memory." The southeast face features a small bust of Abraham Lincoln, and the northwest face has a bronze inset depicting George Washington.

The first name listed on the southeast face is Maj. Gen. Joseph Mansfield, a Middletown native who was killed in the battle of Antietam. His grave and a nearby GAR monument can be found in the city's Indian Hill Cemetery.

The infantry statue atop the monument was cast in Chicopee, Mass., and bears the name of sculptor Melzar Mosman on the northwest base of the statue. Other works by Mosman include monuments in Danielson, as well as the figures on the Civil War monuments in New Haven's East Rock Park and Bridgeport's Seaside Park.

The supplier of the monument is not known, but presumably was Middletown's Fox-Becker Granite Company.

The base of the Soldier's Monument is surrounded by four Confederate cannons.

Nearby Monuments
Across Main Street, two large plaques honor Middletown residents who served in World War I. The plaques can be seen on the outside walls of an armory building that was later converted into an inn.

Veterans' Memorial Green, Middletown

A collection of monuments on Veterans' Memorial Green along Washington Street in Middletown honors those who served in the Civil War, the two World Wars, Korea and Vietnam.

A 1904 monument near the western end of the green honors the 24th Regiment Connecticut Volunteers, a unit that fought primarily in Louisiana. The monument features a column flanked by two curved benches and a sphere topped by a bronze eagle. The front (north) face of the monument bears the numeral 24 in a wreath, and lists the battle of Port Hudson.

A bronze plaque is inscribed with a dedication reading, "Erected by members of the 24th C.V., citizens of Middletown and [the] state of Connecticut 1904."

The west face of the monument lists the battle of Irish Bend, Louisiana. The south face lists the battle of Donaldsonville, Louisiana, and bears a plaque honoring about 75 members of the regiment. The east face lists the battle of Baton Rouge.

The monument was supplied by the Fox-Becker Granite Company of Middletown.

Nearby Monuments

Further east on the green, a polished black granite monument
honors local veterans of the Korean and Vietnam wars. Four large
panels bear service emblems and the years of the two conflicts, as
well as a dedication, "Beyond the far Pacific to the rim of Asia they
went – twice in a generation – to risk all for honor and freedom."
The monument also lists two residents killed in Vietnam.

Further east, a white obelisk honors 37 soldiers and sailors who
died in World War I. A plaque on the south side honors the war
heroes, while a plaque on the west side lists seven battles.

Nearby, three polished granite panels honor the service of World
War II veterans. The front bears the dedications, "Their devotion and
sacrifices contributed to final victory," and "Dedicated to the men
and women of Middletown who served in the armed forces of their
country in time of war." The monument also bears a bronze plaque
with three columns listing residents who were lost in the war.

Gen. Joseph Mansfield and
GAR Monuments, Middletown

U.S. Civil War Major General Joseph K. F. Mansfield and other local Civil War veterans are honored with monuments in Middletown's Indian Hill Cemetery.

Gen. Mansfield was born in New Haven in 1803, and was a career Army officer who served in the Corps of Engineers after graduating from West Point. During his military service, Mansfield lived in Middletown, and his Main Street home has been restored by the Middlesex County Historical Society.

Mansfield was mortally wounded during the Battle of Antietam on Sept. 17, 1862, and was returned to Middletown for burial.

An ornate sandstone monument honoring Mansfield and his family is located in a central area of Indian Hill Cemetery, which rises above Middletown's Washington Street (Route 66).

An inscription on the front (west) face of the Mansfield monument bears the general's name, date and place of death, and his age. The inscription on the east face honors his wife, Louisa, who died in 1880. Inscriptions on the north and south faces list the couple's two children.

The sarcophagus-shaped monument is topped by an elaborate carving of a U.S. flag, a sword and a hat.

Not far from the Mansfield monument is an 1884 monument erected by the local Grand Army of the Republic post in a section of the cemetery reserved for Civil War veterans.

The granite monument depicts an infantry solider holding a rifle. A dedication on the front (east) face reads, "To the memory of deceased soldiers & sailors by Mansfield Post No. 53, Department of Conn. G.A.R., A.D. 1884."

The other three faces of the monument are generally plain, other than Corps emblems just beneath the base supporting the figure.

The area around the monument has a number of graves of Civil War veterans.

Soldiers' Monument, Portland

Portland honors its Civil War heroes with an 1872 obelisk made from local brownstone.

The front (northwest) face of the obelisk bears the dedication, "Erected May 30, 1872, by the town of Portland to the memory of her brave sons who gave their lives in defence of the Union during the War of the Rebellion 1861-5."

The northwest face also lists the names, regimental affiliations, and the date and location of death for seven residents lost in the conflict. The monument's northwest face also bears a carved eagle atop the Connecticut and U.S. shields, and lists the battles of Atlanta and Gettysburg.

The southwest face bears the names of seven residents, and lists the battles of Cassville (Georgia) and Chancellorsville (Virginia.) The southeast face lists eight names as well as the battles of Resaca and Peach Tree Creek (both in Georgia). The northeast face lists seven names and the battles of Silver Run (Maryland) and Bentonville (North Carolina.)

The monument was supplied by James Batterson of Hartford.

Portland was a leading producer of brownstone, a form of sandstone that was a popular building material in the late 19th and early 20th centuries.

The Portland Soldiers' Monument stands on a triangular green at the intersection of Main Street (Route 17) and Bartlett Street. The green also features two Civil War cannons. One cannon was manufactured in 1862, and the other was made a year earlier. The 1862 cannon barrel has an impressive cluster of insect nests that we chose not to explore in detail.

War Memorial, East Hampton

East Hampton honors veterans of World War I and earlier conflicts with plaques on a boulder in its historic village center.

The undated war memorial, at the intersection of Main Street and Summit Street (Route 196), honors veterans of World War I, the Spanish-American War, the Civil War, the War of 1812 and the American Revolution with plaques mounted on a large boulder.

The south face of the monument bears a plaque with a dedication reading, "In honor of East Hampton men and women who served their country in the World War 1917-1918."

Below the dedication, the plaque lists about 141 names, and indicates four who were killed in the war.

On the monument's west face, a plaque honoring Civil War veterans bears a dedication reading, "To perpetuate the memory of the men from this township in the Civil War, 1861-1865, fought to preserve the Union."

The plaque also lists about 109 residents who served in the war.

The monument's north face honors a dozen residents who served in the Spanish-American War.

The east face of the monument honors veterans of the American Revolution and the War of 1812 with a plaque reading, "To the memory of the patriot men of Chatham who bravely bore their part in the War of the American Revolution and the War of 1812 to establish firmly the foundations of our republic and to preserve the liberties which we have inherited."

The reference to Chatham reflects East Hampton's former name. The town separated from Middletown in 1767, and was known as Chatham until it adopted the East Hampton name in 1915.

The fact that the Civil War and Spanish-American War plaques refer to "this township" probably reflects the name change in the intervening years.

The monument stands in East Hampton's Belltown Historic District, which is listed on the National Register of Historic Places.

East Hampton was a leading center for bell production during the 19th Century and the early 20th. According to the 1860 census, nearly half of East Hampton's 1,766 residents, many of whom were Irish immigrants, worked for one of the town's 30 bell factories.

Soldiers' Monument, Moodus

East Haddam honors its Civil War veterans with a monument on the Moodus Green.

The monument, dedicated in 1900, features a granite infantryman facing south. A dedication on the monument's south face reads, "In honored memory of the brave defenders of our country in its hour of peril 1861-1865."

The south face also lists the Battle of Gettysburg.

The east face lists the Battle of Antietam, and honors 10 residents lost in the war. The north face lists Appomattox and 14 residents, and the west face lists the Battle of Petersburg (Virginia) and the names of 10 residents.

Because the granite panels inscribed with the names were polished, the inscribed names are difficult to discern today.

The monument's square base supports a round column draped with banners. The column is topped by the infantry figure, whose left foot extends slightly beyond the base.

The monument stands on the small green at the intersection of East Haddam-Moodus Road (Route 149) and Plains Road (Route

151) in the Moodus section of East Haddam.

Nearby Monuments

Immediately south of the Soldiers' Monument is a memorial honoring residents lost in World War I. A bronze honor roll plaque is topped with a large eagle, the United States shield, several flags, and emblems representing the Army and the Navy.

The plaque honors one resident who died in service during the war. In the section listing Army veterans, 67 residents are honored. The monument further lists 22 residents who served with the Navy, and one who provided support services with the Y.M.C.A.

Veterans' Memorial, Old Saybrook

Old Saybrook honors its Civil War veterans with a simple monument in Riverside Cemetery.

The undated monument stands in a small traffic island near the cemetery's Sheffield Street entrance. A dedication on its front (south) face reads, "In memory of our comrades who served in the War of the Rebellion. Erected by the veterans of Old Saybrook."

The monument's base lists the years during which the Civil War took place.

The monument's reference to the "War of the Rebellion" likely indicates the monument was erected in the late 19th Century. By the early 20th Century, the conflict was more commonly described as the Civil War.

The monument has no lettering on its other faces. A smaller, more modern granite marker at the base of the monument bears the inscription, "Veterans' Memorial." Several Civil War veterans are buried near the monument.

Nearby Monuments

A short distance southwest of the cemetery, three monuments in front of Town Hall honor the veterans of the 20th Century's wars. A 1926 monument honoring the service of World War I veterans bears a dedication on its front (west) face reading, "In memory of Old Saybrook's sons who served." The monument's east face has a plaque with two columns of names listing local veterans, organized by service branches. The monument is topped by a bronze eagle.

Near the World War monument, a granite monument dedicated in 1961 honors local war heroes. A dedication near the top of the monument reads, "Erected by the citizens of Old Saybrook in memory of her sons who died at war."

Beneath that dedication, the monument lists heroes and the wars in which they were lost. One person is listed for World War I; 15 for World War II; two for Korea, and one for Vietnam.

A polished granite monument in front of three flagpoles bears the POW-MIA logo. An eternal flame flickers in front of the monument.

NEW LONDON COUNTY

Soldiers' and Sailors' Monument, New London

A privately funded, 50-foot obelisk in downtown New London honors the city's Civil War veterans.

The 1896 Soldiers' and Sailors' Monument features an obelisk with alternating granite bands topped by an allegorical figure representing Peace. A dedication on its front (west) face reads, "Presented to their native city by the sons of Joseph Lawrence, May 6, 1896." (Joseph Lawrence was a New London whaler, and he and his family also founded business and philanthropic ventures.)

The west face also bears a bronze plaque with the Connecticut and New London seals.

The dedication on the east face reads, "In memory of New London's soldiers and sailors who fought in defence of their country. Erected on the site of her first fort, fortified 1691, dismantled 1777."

The south face honors the city's proud naval heritage with a statue of a mariner holding a telescope and a rope. The obelisk is engraved with the names of several Civil War, War of 1812 and American Revolution battleships. The south face also lists the word "Defence" as well as the "Don't give up the ship" motto (the dying words of USS Chesapeake commander James Lawrence (who does not appear to be related to the New London Lawrences)).

The north face features a Union soldier in a traditional pose, with an upright rifle between his hands. The obelisk above him is engraved with several Civil War and American Revolution battle sites, including Gettysburg, Port Hudson (Louisiana), Fredericksburg (Virginia), Antietam (Maryland), Groton and Bunker Hill.

The west face is also inscribed, "Erected by Sebastian D. Lawrence," who was one of Joseph Lawrence's sons and president of the National Whaling Bank. The family also helped found the city's Lawrence & Memorial Hospital.

The monument, near the intersection of State and Water streets, is the centerpiece of downtown's Parade plaza. Renovations to the Parade have opened views of New London Harbor from the plaza, as well as downtown from Union Station (the building east of the monument). The area also features a red schoolhouse in which Nathan Hale taught.

21st Regiment Monument, New London

The 21st Regiment, Connecticut Volunteer Infantry, is honored with a granite obelisk in New London's Williams Memorial Park.

The monument, near the north corner of the park, was dedicated in 1898 to honor members of the 21st regiment, which was founded in 1862 and recruited primarily from eastern Connecticut towns.

The front (north) face of the monument is inscribed, "21st. Regt. Conn. Vol.," and the unit's service years of 1862-1865 are listed. A little higher on the north face, a dedication reads, "Erected Sept. 5, 1898, by the state of Connecticut in honor of her citizen soldiers." (The monument was dedicated on Oct. 20, 1898.)

The north face also lists the unit's service at the battles of Drewry's Bluff and Petersburg, and the west face lists battles of Fort Harrison and Richmond. The south face lists the battles of Fair Oaks and Suffolk, and the east face honors the battles of Fredericksburg and Cold Harbor. (All the listed battles took place in Virginia.)

Survivors of the regiment originally voted to place the monument in Willimantic, but a disagreement over the monument's location led to the monument being erected at the New London site.

G.A.R. Civil War Monument, New London

One of New London's three monuments to its Civil War veterans anchors a burial plot in the city's Cedar Grove Cemetery.

The ornate monument, near the cemetery's main entrance, features an infantryman standing atop a multi-staged pedestal. A dedication on the front (north) face of the monument reads, "In memory of our comrades 1861-1865."

The front face also bears the inscription "Erected by W.W. Perkins Post, No. 47, G.A.R.," and features a medal symbolizing the Grand Army of the Republic, the Civil War veterans' organization.

The monument is not dated, and information about its construction has not come to light. Based on the ornate decorative elements on the pedestal, the Connecticut Historical Society estimated a dedication date around 1900.

The monument stands at the center of a triangular plot featuring 33 headstones of Civil War veterans. A plot with veterans of more recent conflicts stands south of the Civil War plot, and the prominence of Naval veterans reflects New London's maritime heritage.

A tree just east of the plot was planted by the local Woman's Relief Corps, a G.A.R. auxiliary organization. A different WRC branch erected the nearby Civil War monument in Stonington.

The G.A.R. Post was named after William W. Perkins, a New London resident and first lieutenant in the Tenth Regiment of the Connecticut Volunteer Infantry who was killed while fighting near Kinston, North Carolina.

Gray Soldiers' Monument, Groton

A monument next to the Fort Griswold battlefield honors Groton's Civil War veterans.

The Gray Soldiers' Monument was a posthumous gift by Robert A. Gray, a Groton native and Civil War veteran who received a Medal of Honor for courage during fighting at Drewry's Bluff, Virginia.

The monument, which features an infantryman standing atop a granite base, bears a dedication on its front (south) face reading, "Erected by Robert A. Gray and dedicated to the memory of his brave comrades who offered their lives for their country in the war of 1861-1865."

The south face also bears the Connecticut and United States shields near its base, and also honors the battle of Fredericksburg, Va. The east face lists the battle of Port Hudson, La. Gettysburg is listed on the north face, and Drewry's Bluff on the west face.

The monument was dedicated July 4, 1916, thanks to Gray's posthumous donation. Gray, a Groton stonecutter, had served with the 21st Regiment, Connecticut Volunteer Infantry.

The monument, near the corner of Park Avenue and Smith Street, stands almost in the shadow of the Groton Battle Monument and museum in Fort Griswold State Park.

The monument was supplied by the Smith Granite Works in nearby Westerly, R.I., and may have been among the last Civil War monuments purchased from the firm.

Gray's unit is honored with a monument in downtown New London's Williams Memorial Park.

Soldiers' Monument, Mystic

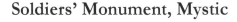

Mystic's Civil War Veterans are honored with an 1883 monument on a downtown traffic island.

The monument, featuring an infantry soldier atop a granite base, sits near the intersection of East Main Street and Broadway Avenue. A dedication on its front (northwest) face reads, "Dedicated to the brave sons of Mystic who offered their lives to their country in the War of the Rebellion, 1861-1865."

Connecticut and United States seals are inscribed into the front face, which also features a wreath and lists the Battle of Antietam.

The northwest face lists the battle of Port Hudson, Louisiana, and the northeast face lists the battle of Gettysburg and the southeast face lists the battle of Drury's Bluff (Virginia). Other than ornamental wreathes near the top of the pedestal, the monument is relatively subdued.

Mystic's monument is also known for a couple of accidents that took place during its 1883 dedication. Several veterans were burned and bruised as they marched near a cannon, loaded with blanks, that was fired despite the vets' proximity. In addition, a crowded grandstand collapsed, but fortunately this incident did not produce any injuries.

The monument was funded by Charles Henry Mallory, who operated a steamship line in New York. Mallory's father, Charles, was a wealthy Mystic shipbuilder and whaler.

The granite for the monument, like that used in many Connecticut Civil War monuments, was quarried in nearby Westerly, R.I.

Woman's Relief Corps Monument, Stonington

Stonington honors its Civil War veterans with a large granite monument in Evergreen Cemetery.

The boulder-shaped monument was dedicated in 1923, a relatively late date for a Civil War commemoration. A somewhat-faded dedication on the monument's front (north) face reads, "Erected by the W.R.C. to the brave sons of Stonington who fought in the War of 1861-1865."

The W.R.C. refers to the Woman's Relief Corps, an organization affiliated with the Grand Army of the Republic. The monument also features an inscribed GAR logo on its front face.

The monument stands at the center of a veterans' plot that includes four Civil War headstones at its corners. One honors a soldier who was killed at the battle of Port Hudson, Louisiana, in 1863, and another honors one who was killed in Fredericksburg, Virginia, in 1862. The other two headstones honor veterans who passed away after the war.

Soldiers' Monument, Ledyard

Ledyard honors its Civil War heroes with a granite obelisk outside one of the town's libraries.

The monument was erected in 1873 to honor Ledyard residents killed in the conflict. A dedication on the monument's front (north) face reads, "In honor of the men of Ledyard who fought for the preservation of the Union in the war of 1861-5. Erected July 4, A.D. 1873, by Ledyard Bill."

The north face also features a raised United States shield and two crossed swords. The south, east and west faces bear the names of 29 Ledyard residents killed in the Civil War.

The monument was donated by Ledyard Bill, a local resident who prospered in the publishing industry in Kentucky and New York. Bill later served as a legislator in Massachusetts.

A short walk away from the Civil War monument, a collection of monuments honors Ledyard's veterans of other wars. A bronze plaque affixed to a boulder honors 32 residents who served in World War I and four who were killed.

Inscriptions on other boulders honor veterans of the American

Revolution, World War II, Korea and Vietnam.

About a quarter-mile north of these monuments, an undated memorial in front of Town Hall honors Ledyard's war veterans.

Soldiers' Monument, Preston

Preston honors the service of local veterans in the Civil War and World War I with a monument on Jewett City Road (Route 164).

The 1898 Soldiers' Monument, which also marks the birthplace of American Revolution general Samuel Mott, stands in front of the former town library building just south of the intersection of Route 164 with Shetucket Turnpike (Route 165).

A dedication on the monument's front (northwest) side reads, "In grateful memory of those citizens of the Town of Preston who served their country in arms in the war for the preservation of the Union."

The northwest face also features a raised United States shield flanked by the years when the Civil War was fought.

The southwest side bears an inscription reading, "From this town, obedient to the call of patriotism and humanity, went forth one hundred and fifty men."

An inscription on the northeast side reads, "Erected in token of filial gratitude and affection for their early home and to commemorate the patriotic devotion of friends & neighbors of their youth by Charles and Lucius Brown, 1898."

The southeast side has an inscription reading, "This monument marks the dwelling place of General Samuel Mott, eminent citizen, upright magistrate, soldier of the Revolution, friend of Washington."

Mott was an engineer who served at Fort Ticonderoga in New York as well as forts in New London and Groton.

On the monument's northwest face, a 1921 plaque lists about 50 residents who served in World War I.

The land on which the monument and the former library stand, now the home of the Preston Historical Society, was donated by the Brown family along with the monument. The monument and the library were both dedicated on November 25, 1898.

The site also features two mortar cannons as well as pyramids of cannonballs.

The monument, supplied by the Smith Granite Company of Westerly, Rhode Island, was restored in 2000.

A spring-fed horse fountain donated in 1918 by retired inventor DeLambre Bates stands a short walk southwest of the Soldiers' Monument site.

The Soldiers' Monument, Norwich

A large monument to soldiers killed in the Civil War stands near the northern end of the Chelsea Parade green in Norwich.

The 1875 monument features a caped infantryman standing with two hands wrapped around the barrel of his rifle. The soldier is looking downward and to his left, making him appear a bit more reflective than the average monument figure.

The 12-foot figure, larger than those atop most of the state's Civil War monuments, stands on an eight-sided column with ornate decorative elements. The front (south) face bears the Connecticut and U.S. shields just below the soldier's feet.

Four of the eight columns bear plaques listing an estimated 160 names and regimental affiliations of local residents who were killed in the war.

The monument, supplied by James Batterson of Hartford, is surrounded by an iron fence that features four matching granite corners bearing the U.S. shield on the outer faces.

Near the south side of the monument's base, a smaller granite marker indicates a time capsule was buried in 1959 to mark the city's

300th anniversary. The time capsule is scheduled to be opened in 2059.

Nearby Monuments

A small triangular park just north of the Soldiers' Monument in Norwich features monuments to the major wars of the 20th Century as well as to an early American who helped settle the design of the U.S. flag.

The area between Broadway and Washington Street, near the Chelsea Parade park, features a granite and bronze monument to the first World War, as well as granite monuments honoring those lost in World War II, Korea and Vietnam, and Vietnam-era POWs/MIAs.

The south end of the park, along William Street, features a granite marker bearing a dedication to those who were lost in "all wars, actions and conflicts." The marker contains an eternal flame enclosed in glass.

A nearby Freedom Tree is dedicated to a local service member captured or reported missing in 1973.

In September of 2013, a memorial was dedicated to honor two local servicemen who were killed serving in Iraq.

A small rock north of these monuments bears a plaque dedicated to Capt. Samuel Chester Reid (1783-1861), a Norwich native who commanded a privateer ship during the War of 1812 and who helped design the 1818 version of the United States flag. The 1818 flag established the convention of adding a star to represent each state (the nation had 20 states at the time, but the flag had 15 stars and 15 stripes) while retaining 13 stripes to represent the original colonies.

Andersonville Memorial, Norwich

A large Civil War cannon is featured in a section of Norwich's Yantic Cemetery dedicated to veterans of the conflict, including nine residents who died as prisoners of war in the Confederate prison at Andersonville, Georgia.

The Norwich veterans who died in the prison were reinterred in Yantic Cemetery on February 1, 1866. The nine graves are arranged in a circular pattern, and several other veterans of the Civil War and later conflicts were added to the area.

A marker near the cannon explains that 15 Norwich residents died in Andersonville. Norwich, the first northern city to retrieve its Andersonville dead, sent representatives to the site after the war. Only the 10 who could be identified were returned to their native city. Nine were reburied in Yantic Cemetery, and one was reburied in his family's plot in the city's Center Cemetery.

The cannon (a 4.2 inch, 30-pounder Parrott Rifle manufactured in 1862) has been painted several times over the years, but layers of paint have been scraped away on the muzzle and barrel to reveal the manufacturer's markings.

Camp Sumter, the Confederate name for the prison constructed in Andersonville, opened in February 1864 to house Union prisoners of war. The site was enlarged in June of that year, and by August, more than 33,000 prisoners were being confined in a 26.5-acre site largely without shelter or sanitary facilities.

By the end of the war, nearly 13,000 Union soldiers had died from disease, malnutrition and exposure to the elements.

The site of Camp Sumter is maintained by the National Park Service. The site also features the National Prisoner of War Museum and an active National Cemetery.

An "Andersonville Boy" statue honoring Connecticut residents who died in captivity was erected in 1907 on the former prison site. A contingent of 103 prison survivors traveled to Georgia for the dedication ceremonies. A copy of the statue stands on the grounds of the state capitol complex.

26th Regiment Monument, Norwich

A tall obelisk in the middle of a small Norwich park honors the members of the 26th Regiment, Connecticut Volunteer Infantry, who served in the Civil War in late 1862 and mid-1863.

The monument, dedicated in 1902 in Little Plain Park (between

Broadway and Union Street), is an obelisk divided into several sections by ornamental details. A dedication on the monument's south face reads, "To the memory of the 26th Regiment Conn. Volunteer Infantry."

Just above the dedication, the south face also bears the name "Port Hudson" and crossed rifles, symbolizing the regiment's service in the infantry. The monument also features the cross of the 19th Corps, in which the regiment served.

The north face bears some statistics about the unit, listing its original enrollment of 825 members and a breakdown of its 278 casualties: 52 killed in action, 142 wounded and 84 died in service.

Information about the supplier is not readily available. The monument's location in Little Plain Park also marks the site of a reception held when the regiment returned from the war.

A regiment comprised primarily of Norwich residents, the 26th's major engagement was the siege of Port Hudson, Louisiana, between May 21 and July 9, 1863. The capture of Port Hudson, together with that of Vicksburg, Mississippi, a few days earlier, gave Union forces effective control of the Mississippi River and provided an important turning point in the Civil War.

The 26th was organized in Norwich on Nov. 10, 1862, and arrived in New Orleans on Dec. 16. The unit was shifted to the siege of Port Hudson on May 24, 1863, and participated in two ill-fated assaults (on May 27 and June 14) that produced no military benefit for the Union.

When word reached Port Hudson on July 9 that Vicksburg had surrendered to Union forces on July 4, the Confederate leaders at Port Hudson also surrendered.

War Memorials, Lebanon

Lebanon honors its war veterans with several monuments on the green near the intersection of Exeter Road (Route 207) and Norwich-Hartford Turnpike (Route 87).

Near the northern end of the green, in front of Town Hall, is a 1922 monument honoring veterans of five wars that took place between the American Revolution and the First World War.

The monument features a stone cairn, serving as a flagpole base, with plaques on the cairn's four sides honoring local veterans.

The north face of the monument features a plaque with a scene depicting soldiers from the American Revolution, the Civil War and World War I marching together under an American flag.

The west face of the monument bears a plaque honoring those who served during the "Period of the World War" (the reference to war "periods" is uncommon among the state's war memorials).

The plaque reads, "In commemoration of the boys who served in the World War. Not unmindful of their heritage, the mantle of their forefathers fell upon patriotic shoulders. They acquitted themselves with honor and loyalty, cheerfully accepting the sacrifices placed upon them in performance of their duty on land and sea. With no selfish end, they served that the principle of right might be established throughout the world."

The south face of the monument bears a plaque that, along with the years of the Civil War, includes a dedication "...to the memory of our Civil War veterans, who so promptly and willingly responded to the nation's call, serving in eleven different regiments and participating in over a hundred different battles; and to our illustrious and renowned second war governor, William Buckingham, who was born and spent his early life in Lebanon. He performed efficient service in the nation's peril, and was a worthy successor of Connecticut's first war governor."

The lower section of the south plaque also commemorates veterans of the 1898 Spanish-American War with a dedication reading, "In honor of those who served in the Spanish War, assisting an oppressed people to achieve their independence."

The east face honors Lebanon's many contributions to the American Revolution as well as the War of 1812. The dedication in the American Revolution section reads, "In memoriam to our fathers who fought for justice and liberty.

"When the war broke out, this town contributed the one loyal governor, brother Jonathan Trumbull, who among all the governors of the thirteen colonies, was the only one who stood staunch and true to the American cause. Washington relied on him in the most trying circumstances.

"William Williams, one of the signers of the Declaration of Independence, was born in Lebanon, the home of the Council of Safety.

"We take a just pride in the noble achievements of our men who served in the Revolution. They were eminently God-fearing and true patriots."

The east face also has a dedication honoring veterans of the War of 1812: "Revered is the memory of those who participated in the War of 1812, who with honor and loyalty fulfilled the trust dedicated to them by their forefathers."

The plaques were designed by sculptor Bruce Wilder Saville, whose other works included war memorials in Massachusetts, New York and Ohio. The monument was built by a local mason.

Nearby Monuments

An undated memorial near the northeast corner of the green honors Lebanon's veterans of the two World Wars. The World War I section lists 40 names and honors one resident who was killed. The World War II section lists about 135 names and honors seven who were killed.

A 2002 memorial near the northwest corner of the green honors veterans of recent conflicts including Korea, Vietnam, Lebanon, Granada, Panama, Persian Gulf, Somalia, Haiti, Bosnia and Afghanistan.

Union Monument, Colchester

Colchester honors the service of its Civil War veterans with an 1875 monument on the town green.

The town's Union monument stands near the northern end of the green, just south of where Main Street (Route 85) meets Hayward Avenue and Lebanon Avenue (Route 16).

A dedication on the monument's south face reads, "Colchester honors its dead who fell in the War for the Union, 1861-5."

The south face also features a shield with the United States and Connecticut emblems, and an inscription reading, "Not ours but the nation's."

The east and west faces both bear honor rolls listing a total of 44 residents who died in the Civil War. The south face lists the dedication date of September 17, 1875 (the 13th anniversary of the Battle of Antietam).

The monument's decorative elements include arches on the four faces as well as carved cannons in the corners of its base.

The figure atop the monument is, uncommon among Connecticut's Civil War memorials, depicted looking down instead of forward. The figure, holding his hat waist-high, perhaps appears to be mourning his fallen colleagues. The figure's left foot extends beyond the monument's base.

The monument is the work of sculptor George E. Bissell, a Civil War veteran who also created elaborate monuments in Winchester, Salisbury and Waterbury.

Old Stone Church Burial Ground, Niantic

East Lyme's Civil War veterans are honored with a 1926 monument in the historic Old Stone Church Burial Ground.

The cemetery, formed in 1719, also has a number of modern markers honoring the graves of residents who served in the French & Indian War, American Revolution, Civil War, and other conflicts.

The Civil War memorial consists of a bronze plaque mounted on a granite slab atop a small hillside in the cemetery. The plaque, on the monument's east face, bears a dedication reading, "In perpetual remembrance of the men of East Lyme who offered their lives to preserve the Union."

The plaque also lists the names of 91 residents who served in the Civil War, as well as its dedication date of June 14, 1926.

The relatively late dedication makes the East Lyme memorial one of the state's last Civil War monuments with a dedication ceremony that could have been attended by veterans of the conflict.

Old Stone Church Burial Ground is at the intersection of Society and Riverview Roads in the Niantic section of East Lyme.

Union Cemetery, Niantic

East Lyme honors Civil War veterans with a memorial gateway at the entrance to Union Cemetery on East Pattagansett Road.

The memorial gateway features two granite pillars with bronze plaques on their eastern faces listing local Civil War veterans.

Both pillars bear a dedication reading, "Smith Gateway. Erected by the late Flora M. Smith in memory of her father, Frederick Malcolm Smith, Co. C 26th Reg't [Connecticut Volunteer Infantry] and the following citizens of the Town of East Lyme who also volunteered for service in the Civil War 1861-1865."

The south pillar bears 43 names, with symbols identifying about nine residents who were killed in the war, as well as those buried in the cemetery. The plaque also identifies African American troops.

The north pillar has similar information about 42 residents.

Eighteen East Lyme residents were killed during the Civil War.

The plaques are undated, but were dedicated after Flora Smith's death in 1923. Her father served in the 26th Regiment of the Connecticut Volunteer Infantry, which fought primarily in Louisiana in 1862 and 1863. The regiment is honored with a monument in

Norwich.

War Memorial Park, Waterford

Waterford honors veterans of the nation's wars with a collection of monuments in two local parks.

Three monuments are featured in a small green in War Memorial Park on Rope Ferry Road (Route 156), near the intersection with Great Neck Road (Route 213).

A bronze plaque on a 1975 monument honors local residents who served in the American Revolution. The plaque bears a dedication reading, "To honor those patriots from the land now Waterford who courageously responded beginning with the Lexington Alarm in the War of Independence, 1775–1783."

The plaque lists nearly 80 names of residents who served in the revolution. At the time, Waterford, incorporated as a town in 1801, was part of New London.

To the west of the American Revolution memorial, a monument honors Waterford's Civil War and Spanish-American War veterans.

The monument's dedication includes similar language to the American Revolution memorial, praising the courage of residents who served in the conflicts and including the starting and ending dates of the wars.

The Civil War section of the monument includes nearly 110 names, and the Spanish-American War section lists 10 names.

A memorial flagpole next to the monument includes the emblems of the military branches in its base.

At the western end of the green, a World War I monument was dedicated in 1928. The dedication plaque contains three columns of names, and highlights five residents who died during their World War service.

Veterans Memorial Green

A little more than a half-mile east of War Memorial Park, Waterford's veterans are further honored with Veterans Memorial Green on the grounds of Town Hall.

The green, at the intersection of Route 156 and Boston Post Road (Route 1), was dedicated in 1997. A granite monument bears an inscription reading, "Dedicated to all the men and women who served in the armed services of the United States of America." In addition to an engraved eagle, the monument also features bronze service emblems.

The plaza surrounding the memorial, dedicated in 2008, has been designated "a path of honor." The plaza features memorial bricks inscribed with the names of local veterans.

WINDHAM COUNTY

Soldiers' and Sailors' Monument, Brooklyn

Brooklyn honors the memory of local Civil War veterans with a Canterbury Road monument featuring an infantry officer standing atop a granite pillar.

The monument, dedicated in 1888, was designed by sculptor Karl Gerhardt, who was also responsible for the nearby monument honoring American Revolution hero Israel Putnam.

The front (east) face of the Civil War monument bears a dedication, "To the memory of all the brave men of Brooklyn who fought on land or sea for the preservation of the Union." The east face also lists the battles of Antietam and Gettysburg.

The rear (west) face of the monument bears a bronze plaque listing the names of approximately 165 residents who served in the conflict, and also lists the battles of Winchester and Drury's Bluff.

The north face lists battles in New Berne (North Carolina) and Cold Harbor (Virginia), and the south face lists the battles of Petersburg and Cedar Creek (Virginia).

Bronze elements on the monument include the Connecticut state seal as well as emblems honoring artillery and naval units.

The monument was donated to Brooklyn by Thomas S. Marlor, an English native and successful financier who retired to the town in 1869. Marlor also donated the site of the Putnam monument, which was funded by the state.

An 1863 Parrott Rifle cannon has been mounted on a brick base next to the monument.

Nearby Monuments
Revolutionary War hero Israel Putnam is honored with an equestrian monument at his burial site on Canterbury Road.

The monument was dedicated in 1888 to honor Putnam, a Massachusetts native who served with distinction during the French and Indian War and who later abandoned his plow in the field to join the Continental Army when the American Revolution began.

Putnam is depicted directing troops on horseback. His horse faces east, and Putnam is looking toward the north. Granite slabs on the north and south faces bear biographical and inspirational messages that were inscribed on Putnam's original headstone.

Upon his death in 1790, Putnam was buried in an aboveground tomb in Brooklyn's South Cemetery. Over the years, souvenir hunters had removed fragments of the headstone and the overall condition of the tomb was deemed unsuitable for General Putnam.

Sculptor Karl Gerhardt, also responsible for the nearby Soldiers' and Sailors' Monument as well as Civil War monuments in New York and New Jersey, was chosen to create a monument that would provide a new home for Putnam's remains. Putnam was placed in a sarcophagus in the base, and the original headstone inscription was recreated on the monument. (The original headstone was put on display in the state capitol.)

North of the monument, a plaque on a boulder marks the site of Putnam's Brooklyn farm and tavern.

Just north of the Civil War and Putnam monuments, Brooklyn has erected a monument to local residents who served in World War II, Korea and Vietnam. The World War II monument features five granite panels listing the residents who served, as honoring seven who died in the conflict. Separate panels, dedicated in 2000, honor the service of residents in Korea and Vietnam.

A bit further north on Canterbury Road, a plaque on a boulder honors residents who served in World War I. The plaque contains about 72 names, and honors three residents who died in the war.

Soldiers' and Sailors' Monument, Danielson

An 1878 monument in the Danielson section of Killingly honors the service of local residents in the Civil War.

The understated Soldiers' and Sailors' Monument features a bronze infantry solider standing atop a four-sided granite base.

The front (northeast) face of the monument bears the dedication, "Erected AD 1878 by the Women's Monument Association and Town of Killingly in honor of the soldiers and sailors who served in the War of 1861 for the preservation of the Union."

The front also bears the Connecticut seal, and the top of the granite base has a small facade adorned with engraved ivy leaves.

The rear side of the monument bears the U.S. shield, and the left and right sides display ornamental wreaths.

Unlike many Civil War monuments in the state, the Danielson monument does not list individual soldiers lost in the war or major battles in which area residents or regiments fought.

The monument stands in Davis Park, at the intersection of Main Street (Route 12) and Broad Street.

A 30-pounder Parrott rifle cannon has been mounted in front of the monument. The cannon bears an 1862 manufacturing date, as well as the initials of the West Point Foundry in Cold Spring, New York. A cannonball pyramid originally stood in front of the cannon, but has since been removed (most likely during a wartime scrap metal drive).

Nearby Monuments

Davis Park also has monuments honoring local residents who fought in the World Wars and Desert Storm. The World War monument, near the southwest corner of the park, is a large boulder topped with a bronze eagle. A plaque on the front face bears four columns listing local residents who served in the conflict, with a section honoring two residents who were killed.

Killingly's World War II monument features a granite slab flanked by two square columns. A plaque on the central slab lists 34 residents killed in the conflict.

The park's Desert Storm monument lists 49 men and women who served in the conflict, and one who was killed.

Davis Park was donated to Killingly in 1893 by Edwin W. Davis, a Danielson native who founded retail stores and banks in Iowa and Colorado. He requested the new park be named for his parents.

Soldiers' Monument, Putnam

Putnam honors local Civil War veterans with a monument in a small park at the corner of Grove Street (Route 12) and Ring Street.

The dedication on the monument's front (east) face reads, "To the memory of the soldiers and sailors of Putnam and vicinity who fought for the preservation of the Union 1861 – 1865."

The bottom of the base is also stamped with the years of the Civil War, and a bronze Grand Army of the Republic medal appears just below the infantryman's feet.

The north and south faces of the monument's base feature raised cannons symbolizing artillery units, and the west face features crossed rifles to honor the infantry. Other than the plaque on the front face, the monument does not have additional lettering.

The monument was erected in 1912 by the A.G Warner chapter of the Woman's Relief Corps. The Relief Corps was an auxiliary organization of the Grand Army of the Republic.

The monument was supplied by the Gorham Company of Providence, Rhode Island.

Memorial Plaques, Thompson

Thompson honors veterans of the Civil War, the Spanish-American War and the American Revolution with plaques affixed to boulders in two sections of town.

Civil War and Spanish-American War veterans are memorialized with a plaque on the common on Thompson Road (Route 193), not far from the intersection with Thompson Hill Road (Route 200).

The east face of the plaque bears the inscription, "Dedicated by the Town of Thompson to honor its soldiers of the Civil and Spanish Wars."

The monument lists approximately 235 Civil War veterans as well as eight who served in the Spanish-American War. The monument also carries a dedication reading, "This monument honors equally any soldier whose name has been unintentionally omitted."

The plaque is not dated, and information about its dedication has not been recorded.

In West Thompson Cemetery, also along Route 193, a monument was dedicated in 1916 to honor the 40 veterans of the American Revolution who are buried in the cemetery. A plaque, affixed to a boulder, lists the veterans and the ranks of officers.

TOLLAND COUNTY

Soldiers' Monument, Stafford Springs

Stafford honors its Civil War veterans with a 1924 monument in its downtown Hyde Park.

The Soldiers' Monument in Stafford Springs features a bronze statue on its front (east) face, and is topped by a bronze eagle.

The design reflects its relatively late dedication, nearly 80 years after the end of the Civil War. No battles are listed, and the monument has very little lettering.

The allegorical figure wears a hooded cloak. Her left hand carries a wreath of forget-me-nots to symbolize immortality, along with palm leaves (glory), roses (love) and poppies (eternal rest).

Near the top of the column, the east and west faces display torches along with an excerpt from the Pledge of Allegiance, "One nation indivisible, with liberty and justice for all."

The monument's front face also displays the years of the Civil War inside a wreath. A dedication near the base reads, "The gift of Colonel Charles Warren to the town of his nativity."

The north and south faces bear no lettering, and display torches.

The monument was funded with a bequest from Stafford native Charles Warren, a Civil War veteran who later became a merchant and banker. Warren, who died in 1920, also donated funds for the Warren Memorial Town Hall, which opened in 1924.

The monument was created by sculptor Frederic Wellington Ruckstull, who also created the Confederate Soldiers and Sailors Monument in Baltimore and several busts at the Library of Congress.

Memorial Cannon, Stafford Springs

Stafford Springs honors its Civil War veterans with a large cannon in Stafford Springs Cemetery on Monson Road (Route 32).

The cannon, dedicated in 1897, bears an inscription on its south (left) face reading, "A tribute to the patriotism of the men who went to the defence of the country from Stafford in the War of the Rebellion. The present bequeaths to the future the remembrance of the heroic past."

The west face has an inscription reading, "Veterans 1861-1865."

The north face bears an inscription reading, "Erected by Winter Post No. 44, G.A.R., assisted by the Woman Relief Corps, and the Sons of Veterans in honor of their comrades. Dedicated May 30, 1897."

The north face of the monument's base also highlights the donation of the surrounding veterans plot by Orrin Converse, a local attorney and officer of the Stafford Springs Savings Bank.

The cannon, a 32-pounder Rodman Gun, was cast in 1850.

Soldiers' Monument, Union

The Town of Union honors its Civil War veterans and their mothers with a monument on the town green.

The monument, dedicated in 1902, features a cannon (which may be a replica) resting on a concrete base. A small cannonball pyramid rests in front of the monument.

A dedication on the southeast side of the monument's base reads, "Dedicated in grateful memory to the mothers who gave their sons, to the soldiers who gave their lives, and to those who, daring to die, survived the War of the Rebellion 1861-1865."

The expression of gratitude toward the soldiers' mothers is uncommon, and perhaps unique among Civil War memorials.

The northwest face of the monument bears a plaque listing 66 Union residents who served in the Civil War.

Somewhat unusually, the honor rolls lists John W. Corbin as well as his substitute, Frank Walker. Corbin had enlisted in the 22nd Regiment of the Connecticut Volunteer Infantry, but arranged for the substitute (who was also from Union) after his father became ill.

Corbin's family donated the plaques, and Corbin presented the monument to the town during the dedication ceremonies.

The southwest face of the Union monument lists 10 members of the local GAR post, as well as the monument's 1902 dedication date.

If the cannon is real, its foundry markings are hidden under paint, and its barrel has been filled with concrete.

Behind the monument, a 1978 CT Historical Commission marker provides a brief introduction to the history of Union, which was incorporated in 1734 and was the last town in the state to be settled east of the Connecticut River.

Near the monument, a plaque marks a time capsule scheduled to be opened on the town's 250th anniversary in 2034.

War Memorials, Ellington

Ellington honors its veterans and war heroes with a pair of monuments on the town green.

Veterans of World War I and earlier conflicts are honored with a granite monument, dedicated in 1926, near the intersection of Maple Street (Route 140) and Main Street (Route 286).

A bronze marker on the monument's east face bears the inscription, "Ellington Remembers," and includes seals of Connecticut, the United States and the town.

The plaque's east face lists residents who served in the American Revolution and World War I, and highlights three residents who died during their World War I service.

The west face of the monument also bears the seals seen on the east face. A bronze plaque lists Ellington residents who served in Colonial era wars in 1675 and 1763, the War of 1812, the Mexican-American War in 1846, the Civil War (referred to as the "War of the Rebellion"), and the Spanish-American War.

The Civil War section includes the names of nearly 150 residents.

Immediately west of the memorial, a monument honors Ellington's veterans of later wars. An inscription on the monument's east face reads, "In memory of those who served their country. World

War II, Korea, Vietnam, Grenada, Lebenon [sic], Panama, Desert Storm, Desert Shield."

Further west on the green, a symbolic Liberty Pole was erected in 1975. Liberty Poles were used before the American Revolution as gathering spots and to invite people to take part in discussions or protests. In many communities, patriots would display a banner on a pole to summon residents.

A small granite marker near the Liberty Pole marks the location of Ellington's first meetinghouse, which was built in 1739.

Memorial Building, Rockville

Vernon honors its veterans with a memorial hall and several monuments in the heart of its Rockville section.

Construction began for Memorial Hall in 1889, and the building was finished a year later.

The building originally contained a meeting hall for the local Grand Army of the Republic chapter, a courtroom and municipal offices.

The former GAR meeting space is occupied today by the New

England Civil War Museum, and the building continues to host municipal offices and a legislative chamber.

The brownstone and brick building, on Park Street, features a number of large arched windows and ornamental details.

The west side of the Memorial Building, for example, includes large stained glass windows on the second floor. The windows are topped on the exterior with brownstone insets displaying an eagle flanked by the Connecticut and United States shields.

The southeast corner features a tower topped by a turret with large windows and copper ornamentation at its peak.

A smaller United States shield can be seen near the archway over the building's front entrance.

A plaque in the building's lobby commemorates Rockville native Gene Pitney, a singer and songwriter who was inducted into the Rock & Roll Hall of Fame in 2002.

Nearby Monuments

Immediately across Park Street from the Memorial Building, a collection of monuments honors Vernon's veterans of the World Wars, Korea and Vietnam.

The central monument bears an inscription reading, "Dedicated to the honor and memory of the men and women of the Town of Vernon who so gallantly served their country in World Wars."

To the west of the World War memorial, a monument honors Vernon residents who served in Vietnam. The granite monument bears the names of seven residents who died in the war.

To the east, a monument honors Vernon's Korean War veterans, and commemorates one resident killed during the conflict.

At the eastern end of the park, a fountain honors William T. Cogswell, a 19th century builder who published a history of Rockville in 1872. The memorial is a 2005 copy of a fountain erected in 1883 by Cogwell's cousin, a San Francisco dentist and ardent temperance advocate. The San Francisco Cogswell erected at least nine fountains in different cities depicting himself, and inscriptions on the base advocated temperance.

Soldiers' Monument, Talcottville

A brownstone monument in the Talcottville section of Vernon honors eight local residents who died during Civil War service.

The monument, in Mount Hope Cemetery, was dedicated in 1869 and restored in 2008. The monument stands on a hill near the cemetery's Elm Hill Road entrance.

The base of the monument's front (south) face bears a dedication reading, "Erected to the memory of the soldiers from this place who gave their lives to their country in the War Against the Rebellion."

The south face also honors two Vernon residents who died during in the war. Frank E. Stoughton, who served in the 14th Regiment of the Connecticut Volunteer Infantry, enlisted in July of 1862 and was wounded during the Battle of Gettysburg. Stoughton was discharged due to disability in 1865, and died on January 1, 1866.

Horace Hunn, who served in the 16th Regiment, was wounded during the Battle of Antietam and died in a hospital on October 12, 1862. He is buried in the Antietam National Cemetery.

The 16th Regiment was formed in July of 1862 and left for Washington on August 29, 1862. The regiment saw its first action during the Battle of Antietam when the unit, barely trained, fought in the 40-Acre Cornfield.

The 16th sent 779 men into combat, and 43 were killed and 161 were wounded. A monument honoring the regiment was dedicated on the Antietam battlefield in 1894.

The east face of the Talcottville monument honors Philip F. Foster of Vernon, another member of the 16th Regiment killed at Antietam. Foster is also buried in the Antietam National Cemetery.

The east face also honors Henry S. Loomis of Vernon, who drowned in the Potomac on April 24, 1865 (a little over two weeks after Lee's surrender at Appomattox).

The north face honors two other members of the 16th Regiment: Alonzo Hills, who died as a prisoner of war in Charleston, South Carolina, on October 6, 1864; and James Bushnell, who died in a hospital on November 15, 1862.

The west face honors Orrin O. Brown, who served with the 106th Regiment of the New York Volunteer Infantry. Brown died on April 22, 1863, while serving as part of a garrison protecting the Baltimore and Ohio railroad from Confederate raids in western Virginia.

The west face also honors Frances Bantley, a member of the 6th Regiment of the Connecticut Volunteer Infantry. Bantley died in the Confederate prisoner of war camp at Andersonville, Georgia, and is buried in the National Cemetery there.

Civil War Monument, Coventry

Coventry honors its Civil War veterans with a simple monument in Nathan Hale Cemetery on Lake Street.

The undated Civil War monument, near the monument honoring Hale, features a 30-pounder Parrott Rifle on a granite base.

A dedication on the east face of the monument's base reads, "Veterans, 1861-1865."

Next to the cannon is a triangular metal bracket that once held a pyramid of shells for the cannon. The fate of the shells has not been recorded, but many Civil War cannonballs and shells were removed from monuments during World War II and donated to scrap metal drives.

The Coventry Parrott Rifle was forged in 1862 at the West Point Foundry in Cold Spring, New York. Similar cannon from the foundry can be seen near monuments in Derby, Ansonia and other Connecticut towns.

Nathan Hale Monument, Coventry

Nathan Hale is honored in his hometown of Coventry with 45-foot-tall granite obelisk dedicated in 1846 near the entrance to Nathan Hale Cemetery.

A dedication on the monument's east face reads, "Captain Nathan Hale, 1776." The north face has an inscription reading, "Born at Coventry, June 6, 1755."

The west face displays the famous quotation cited as Hale's final words: "I only regret that I have but one life to lose for my country."

The south face reads, "Died at New York, Sept. 22, 1776."

Fundraising for the monument, designed by New Haven architect Henry Austin, began in 1837.

A wayside marker near the monument provides information about Hale's life and the cemetery.

Hale, a Coventry native and Yale graduate, taught in East Haddam and New London before volunteering to serve as a spy in New York in 1776. Hale was captured and hanged by the British, and his body was buried in an unrecorded location.

Hale, designated as Connecticut's official hero in 1985, is honored with statues in New London's Williams Park, the Yale campus, the state capitol, and New Haven's Fort Nathan Hale; and with a bust in

East Haddam. His family's Coventry home is maintained as a museum.

Memorial Green, Hebron

Hebron honors its war veterans with several monuments on its Memorial Green.

The green, near the intersections of Route 66 (Main Street) and Route 85 (Church Street), features four memorials to veterans from the Civil War, the World Wars, Korea and Vietnam.

The newest monument on the green, honoring Hebron residents who died while serving in the Civil War, was dedicated on Memorial Day 2011.

The monument features a granite marker with a dedication on its east face reading, "Hebron Court of Honor. They gave their lives in the Civil War 1861-1865." The monument also lists 10 residents who died during their wartime service.

A small cannon stands next to the monument, which was donated by the Sons of the American Legion.

Behind the Civil War memorial, an undated monument honors

Hebron residents who served in World War II, Korea and Vietnam. The central tablet bears an engraved eagle and an inscription reading, "Dedicated to the men and women from the town of Hebron who served in World War II and the Korean and Vietnam conflicts."

The World War II tablet features three columns of names and highlights five residents who died during the war. The Korea and Vietnam tablet also bears three columns of names.

To the north of this monument, a pink granite memorial honors the five Hebron residents who died during World War II. The monument features an engraved Connecticut shield and an inscription reading, "Hebron Court of Honor. They gave their lives in World War II 1941 – 1945."

Near the south end of the green, a memorial honors Hebron's World War I veterans. A bronze plaque set into a granite boulder bears the simple inscription, "World War Roll of Honor."

The monument highlights one resident killed in the war, and lists two columns of Hebron residents who served.

HARTFORD COUNTY

Standard-Bearer, Glastonbury

A 1913 granite Civil War monument anchors an impressive collection of war memorials on the Glastonbury Green.

A dedication on the front (south) face of the Standard-Bearer monument reads, "Erected in memory of Capt. Frederick M. Barber and the soldiers of Glastonbury who gave their lives for their country, by Mercy Turner Barber, 1913."

The monument honors Barber, who served in the 16th Regiment of the Connecticut Volunteer Infantry, and other Civil War veterans from Glastonbury. Barber died from wounds suffered during the Battle of Antietam.

The east and north faces are blank, but the west face is inscribed with a lengthy dedication reading, "More enduring than this monument will be the memory of their loyal, patriotic devotion to their country. This granite shaft in time will crumble to dust, but the memory of their heroic deeds, the noble sacrifice of their lives, will live in memory's realm 'till time shall be no more."

Atop the monument, the standard-bearer has the flag cradled in his left arm, with his right hand ready to draw a sword in defense of the flag.

Nearby Monuments

The Standard-Bearer is the largest of six monuments on the green. The western-most monument in the collection honors the service of local residents in World War I with a bronze plaque mounted on a granite base. A dedication atop the plaque reads, "In honor of those of the Town of Glastonbury who answered their country's call to serve humanity." The plaque, dedicated in 1924, also bears six columns of names and highlights 16 residents killed in the conflict.

To the immediate right of the World War I monument is the granite base of a monument, now blank, that once held a plaque.

Next to the blank monument is a granite monument honoring U.S. Air Force Sergeant John Lee Levitow, who was awarded the Congressional Medal of Honor during the Vietnam War. A detailed account of his actions appears on a bronze plaque in front of the granite marker.

A monument to the east of the Standard-Bearer honors Korean War veterans, including a local Marine who was killed in the conflict.

The eastern-most monument on the green honors World War II veterans. The monument, dedicated in 1950, lists 27 residents who were killed in the conflict.

Soldiers' Monument, Manchester

Manchester's Civil War veterans are honored with a monument in the city's Center Memorial Park.

The monument features a bronze infantryman standing atop a granite base inscribed with the Connecticut and United States shields. A dedication on the northeast face reads, "In memory of the soldiers of Manchester who died in the War of the Rebellion 1861-1865."

The monument's base is rough-hewn, and free from other inscriptions or dedications. The figure was sculpted by Charles Conrads, who worked for James G. Batterson (the Hartford industrialist who supplied many Civil War monuments in the state).

The monument originally faced southeast, toward the park. In 1965, it was turned around to face the intersection of Main Street (Route 83) and Center Street (Routes 6 and 44).

Manchester's Soldiers' Monument was dedicated on Sept. 17, 1877, the 15th anniversary of the Battle of Antietam, and was cleaned before a 2005 rededication.

Nearby Monuments

A Spanish-American War monument stands a short walking distance west of the Soldiers' Monument, near Manchester's Probate Court. A dedication near the monument's base reads, "A memorial to the boys of Manchester, Conn., who volunteered and served their country in the Spanish American War."

About a half-mile north of the Soldiers' Monument is the city's World War I monument, which stands outside Manchester Memorial Hospital. The monument features a bronze plaque mounted on a boulder near the hospital's Haynes Street entrance.

A dedication on the front (north) face reads, "This tablet is erected in memory of these men of Manchester who made the supreme sacrifice in the World War 1917-1918." Below the dedication, the monument lists the names of 45 residents killed in the conflict.

The hospital was built in 1920, in part as a response to the 1918 influenza outbreak, and was dedicated to World War I veterans. In 1970, it was rededicated to honor all war veterans.

Soldiers Monument, East Hartford

East Hartford honors its Civil War veterans with an 1868 obelisk erected at the highest point of Center Cemetery.

A dedication on the base of the monument's front (west) face reads, "The Union, it must and shall be preserved." The west face also bears the U.S. and Connecticut shields, and a decorative trophy featuring a flag, crossed rifles, a sword and a haversack. The west face also lists the Andersonville prison camp in Georgia, and the battle of Cold Harbor (Virginia).

Also on the west face, five residents killed during the war are listed by name, regimental affiliation, the location and date of death, and their age.

The south face lists six residents and battles in Sharpsburg (Maryland, where the battle of Antietam took place), and Kingston (Georgia). The base bears the dedication, "All honor to the brave."

The east face lists six residents, the battles of Petersburg and Drury's Bluff (both in Virginia) and the dedication, "We mourn the patriot dead."

The north face provides a tangible reminder of the Civil War's devastating effect on many families and towns. Among the six names listed on the monument, three are from the Flint family: Alvin Flint, who died in 1863 at the age of 58, Alvin Flint, Jr., 17, who was killed in 1862 at Antietam, and George B. Flint, who died in 1864 in Falmouth, Virginia, at the age of 18.

The north face also lists Antietam and Port Hudson (Louisiana), and a dedication reading, "Erected by voluntary subscription to the memory of the brave men who gave up their lives that the republic might live."

A short cannon and a stack of cannonballs appear near the northwest corner of the monument. A deteriorating brownstone eagle was removed from the top of the obelisk in 1996, and replaced with a replica in 2010.

Nearby Monuments

East Hartford honors its World War I heroes with a 1929 statue at the intersection of Central Avenue and Main Street. A dedication on the west face reads, "In honor of the men and women of East Hartford who answered their country's call to service in the World War. To the dead a tribute, to the living a memory, to posterity a token of loyalty to the flag of their country."

A plaque on the monument's east face lists 18 residents who gave their lives in the conflict.

Soldiers' Monument, Enfield

Enfield honors its Civil War and World War I veterans with a granite monument topped by a bronze infantryman.

The Soldiers' Monument, near the corner of Church and North Main streets, was dedicated in 1885 to honor the town's Civil War heroes. A dedication plaque on the monument's front (south) face reads, "In memory of the men of Enfield who, on land and sea, periled their lives for Union and liberty, 1861-1865. Erected by the town of Enfield, A.D. 1885."

A plaque on the east side of the monument lists 10 residents killed in action, 14 who died from wounds, and 15 who died in the Confederate POW camp at Andersonville, Georgia.

The monument's west side features a plaque listing 29 Enfield residents who died during their Civil War service.

The monument's base features four eagles with emblems

representing the artillery, infantry, cavalry and navy.

The north face of the monument honors Enfield's World War I heroes with a bronze plaque dedicated in 1922. The plaque reads, "In memory of those who gave their lives in the great war for world-wide liberty 1917-1919."

The plaque lists eight residents killed in action and five (including a Red Cross nurse) who died in service.

The monument's sculptor, David Richards, created a number of public works including monuments in Lawrence, Mass., and Manchester, N.H., as well as the newsboy statue in Great Barrington, Mass.

The infantryman was cast by the M.J. Power Foundry, which was also responsible for Civil War monuments in Ansonia and Derby.

Veterans' Memorial, Suffield

Suffield honors its veterans with a five-sided granite monument incorporating plaques from an earlier memorial.

The 2003 monument in Veterans' Park, near the intersection of Main Street (Route 75) and Bridge Street, honors Suffield veterans from wars ranging from the French and Indian Wars through recent conflicts in the Persian Gulf.

The monument, topped by a large bronze eagle facing east, features a dedication reading, "In honor of the men and women of Suffield who served in our armed forces in the time of war."

The monument also features two bronze Honor Roll plaques from a 1920 war memorial that list veterans of the French and Indian War, American Revolution, War of 1918, Mexican War, Civil War, Spanish-American War, and World War I.

The granite sections honor veterans of World War II, Korea, Vietnam, and the Persian Gulf.

Soldiers' Monument, Suffield

Suffield honors its Civil War veterans with an 1888 monument near the southern end of the town green.

The Soldiers' Monument bears a dedication on its front (south) face reading, "Suffield erects this memorial in honor of her citizen soldiers who died serving their country that the Union might be preserved. 1861-65."

The monument features a granite infantryman holding a rifle. The soldier's left foot extends over the monument's base.

The monument's east face lists the names and regimental affiliation of 31 Suffield residents lost in the Civil War. The east face also lists Sharpsburg, the Maryland town where the Battle of Antietam was fought in 1862.

The north face bears an intricate state of Connecticut seal and honors Fort Wagner in South Carolina.

The west face displays crossed cannon representing the artillery and lists Andersonville, the Georgia town where a large Confederate prisoner of war camp was built.

The monument was supplied by the Maslen Company of Hartford, and was most likely created in Barre, Vermont.

Memorial Hall, Windsor Locks

Windsor Locks honors its veterans with a granite building that hosts a collection of memorials and a museum.

Memorial Hall, at the corner of Elm Street (Route 140) and Main Street (Route 159), was dedicated in 1891 as a home for the town's Grand Army of the Republic post.

A dedication inscribed near the hall's front entrance reads, "Soldiers' Memorial Hall, built by Charles E. Chaffee and presented by him to J.H. Converse Post, No. 67, G.A.R., in memory of those who went from Windsor Locks and lost their lives in the service of our country in the late Civil War."

The inscription marks a fairly early use of the term "Civil War" to describe the conflict, which is more commonly referred to as the "War of the Rebellion" on Connecticut monuments.

In front of the hall, a 1953 monument honors the service of Windsor Locks residents in the World Wars. The monument's central section lists seven residents lost in World War I and 16 killed in World War II. The left and right sections include an Honor Roll listing the residents who served.

The 1953 monument is flanked by a pair of monuments, dedicated in 1976, honoring the service of Windsor Locks' Korea and Vietnam veterans.

Memorial Hall, which today hosts the town's American Legion post, also features two cannons in front of the building as well as a museum honoring the town's war heroes.

Charles E. Chaffee, who supplied most of the funding for Memorial Hall, was a textile manufacturer who also served as vice president of a bank and president of a bridge and ferry company, and held several municipal offices.

Joseph Converse, for whom the GAR post was named, was a Windsor Locks resident killed during fighting at Cold Harbor, Virginia, in 1864.

Soldiers' and Sailors' Memorial Arch, Hartford

A landmark Bushnell Park arch with two towers and a life-sized frieze honors Hartford's Civil War veterans.

The Soldiers' and Sailors' Memorial Arch, dedicated in 1886, features two medieval towers alongside an archway that spans Trinity Street. A dedication on the east tower (on your right if you stand with your back to the Capitol building) reads, "In honor of the men of Hartford who served, and in memory of those who fell on land and on sea in the War for the Union, their grateful townsmen have raised this memorial."

The monument's west tower has a dedication plaque reading, "During the Civil War, 1861-1865, more than 4,000 men of Hartford bore arms in the national cause, nearly 400 of whom died in the service. Erected 1885."

The monument is dominated by the frieze depicting a variety of scenes that took place during and after the war. The south side of the frieze, by sculptor Caspar Buberl, illustrates the return of Hartford's soldiers after the war. On the eastern side, soldiers and sailors are leaving a ship and are being greeted by family members.

An allegorical figure in the center of the scene represents Hartford. At her feet, the arch is inscribed with the city's Latin motto, post nubila phoebus, which translates as "after clouds, the sun." The motto also reflects the joy and optimism that followed the dark days of the Civil War.

The north frieze, by sculptor Samuel Kitson, illustrates scenes from the war. Ulysses S. Grant is depicted on the frieze's far right.

Just below the frieze, decorative elements honor the infantry (crossed rifles) and cavalry (swords) on the south side, and the Navy and the artillery service on the north side.

The two turrets are also decorated with five figures representing the variety of occupations Connecticut's veterans left behind to fight in the Civil War, as well as a figure on the west turret depicting an emancipated slave. The towers are topped with angels heralding the return of Hartford's soldiers.

The monument, which was dedicated in 1886 on the September 17 anniversary of the Battle of Antietam, originally stood at the southern end of a bridge over the Park River. The river was diverted underground during the 1940s, but the bridge parapets on the east side of the bridge can be seen from the park (just north of the archway).

The monument underwent an extensive renovation in 1988, during which a plaque was attached to the west tower to honor the contributions of African American soldiers in the Civil War. In addition, the terra cotta angels atop the two towers were replaced with bronze replicas.

The monument was designed by George Keller. After his death in 1935, the cremated remains of Keller and his wife, Mary, were interred in the interior of the arch's east tower.

Other Bushnell Park Monuments

Hartford's Spanish-American War veterans are honored with the allegorical Spirit of Victory monument near the intersection of Elm and Trinity streets.

The monument features a winged figure atop the bow of a ship, with an eagle figurehead representing the United States. Victory stands with a torch in her raised right arm, and her left hand holds a shield decorated with the United States flag.

The Spirit of Victory was created by noted sculptor Evelyn Beatrice Longman, who is perhaps best known for Electricity and the Spirit of Communication, the "golden boy" statue that served as a symbol of AT&T for many years. Longman also created decorative elements on the Lincoln Memorial in Washington, and her Connecticut works include the World War monuments in Naugatuck and Windsor.

American Revolution General Israel Putnam is honored with an statue by sculptor John Quincy Adams Ward that was dedicated in 1874. The statue depicts Putnam cradling a sword in his left hand and holding a three-cornered hat in his right hand.

Dental pioneer Horace Wells, an early promoter of the use of anesthesia, is also honored with a statue in the park. The Wells statue, by T.H. Bartlett, was also dedicated in 1874.

A monument along Trinity Street honoring laborers killed on the job was dedicated in 2010.

1st. Conn. Heavy Artillery Monument, Hartford

A 13-inch mortar used in the Civil War was mounted on the grounds of the state capitol in 1902.

The mortar, nicknamed the "Petersburg Express" and "the Dictator," was used in a series of trench-fighting skirmishes near Petersburg, Virginia, and Richmond in 1864 and 1865.

The monument was erected in 1902 to honor the service of the 1st Conn. Heavy Artillery unit, which was formed in 1861 and served in the defense of Washington and several engagements in Virginia before the Petersburg siege.

The mortar has been mounted on a granite base near the intersection of Capitol Avenue and Trinity Place. The south face bears a plaque reading, "This 13-inch sea coast mortar was in actual use by the regiment during the campaign in front of Petersburg 1864-1865 and widely known as the 'Petersburg Express.'"

The west face has a plaque listing the regiment's service dates, and the east face has information about the monument's dedication. The north face bears a bronze Connecticut seal.

Andersonville Boy, Hartford

Connecticut honors Civil War veterans who were held in Confederate prisoner of war camps with a statue on the grounds of the state capitol.

The "Andersonville Boy" statue, dedicated in 1907, honors the state's Civil War POWs. A dedication on the monument's east face reads, "In memory of the men of Connecticut who suffered in Southern military prisons, 1861-1865."

The monument depicts a young soldier wearing a simple frock coat and holding a hat in his left hand.

The monument was created by sculptor Bela Pratt, whose other works include a notable statue of Nathan Hale on the Yale campus in New Haven.

The Hartford statue is a copy of a monument dedicated, also in 1907, at the site of the Andersonville prison camp in Georgia. During the war, nearly 13,000 of the 45,000 Union prisoners held at the camp died from disease and malnutrition. The camp was known for overcrowding and poor sanitary conditions.

A monument in Norwich's Yantic Cemetery honors Civil War veterans from the city who died at Andersonville.

The Old Solider, Hartford

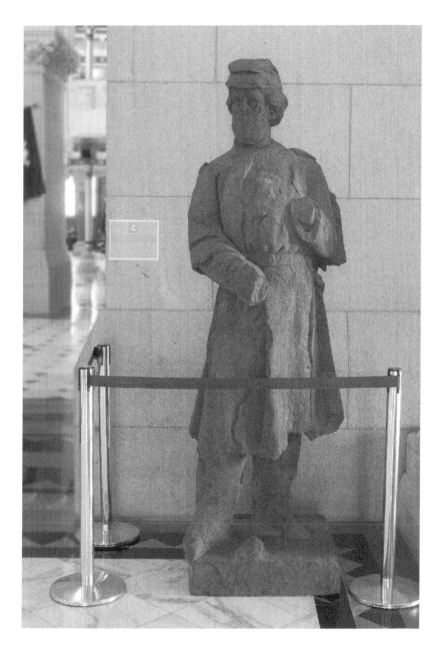

One of the state's newest Civil War monuments is also one of its oldest.

On September 17, 2013, the 151st anniversary of the Battle of Antietam, the "Old Soldier" monument was rededicated and installed in the lobby of the state capitol building in Hartford.

The installation marks the latest stop on a long and often-troubled journey for the brownstone monument, which originally depicted an infantryman holding a rifle. The monument was left behind when James Batterson's New England Granite Works, a leading supplier of Civil War monuments, was sold near the end of the 19th century.

The monument, also known as the Forlorn Soldier, was then displayed in downtown Hartford and moved to Airport Road in 1968. Over the years, vandalism, flooding and exposure to the elements resulted in the removal and erosion of the figure's rifle, hands and face.

As part of the efforts to commemorate the 150th anniversary of the Civil War, the Connecticut Civil War Commemoration Commission led efforts to have the Old Soldier restored and moved to the state capitol building.

Commission co-chair Matthew Warshauer, a Central Connecticut State University historian, suggested at the dedication the name "Old Soldier" was more appropriate than "forlorn."

A legend arose at some point suggesting the figure had been rejected by a town due to the improper placement of his feet and unofficial military posture. More recent research suggests the figure was likely a model used by Batterson's sculptors to create later Civil War monuments, and could have been carved as early as 1866.

Griffin A. Stedman Monument, Hartford

Hartford honors a "typical volunteer soldier" of the Civil War with a monument near the site where many of the state's regiments trained before heading south.

The Griffin A. Stedman monument in the city's Barry Square

neighborhood stands on Campfield Avenue, which was named for the fields in which several of Connecticut's volunteer infantry regiments trained.

Stedman, a Hartford native, was appointed a captain in the 5th Regiment in 1861. He was promoted four times during the war, and was wounded at the Battle of Antietam. He reached the rank of brigadier general before being killed at Petersburg, Virginia, at the age of 26.

Stedman is buried in Hartford's Cedar Hill Cemetery.

The monument, dedicated in 1900, honors Stedman and the Connecticut regiments who camped near the monument before starting their Civil War service.

A dedication on the west face reads, "Griffin A. Steadman, typical volunteer soldier of the Civil War. Captain, Major, Lieutenant Colonel, Colonel, Brigadier General. Born at Hartford, Conn., January 6, 1838. Killed at Petersburg, Va., August 5, 1864." The west face also displays crossed rifles representing the infantry and crossed swords, representing the cavalry.

Gen. Stedman stands atop the monument, facing west with binoculars in his right hand and his left resting near his sword.

A bronze plaque on the south face describes the location of the former regimental camps, and the east face bears a bronze Connecticut shield. The north face has a bronze plaque honoring the units that trained in Hartford (the 5th, 8th, 10th, 14th, 16th, 22nd and 25th). The monument's base also has concrete cannon balls.

The monument was sculpted by Frederick Moynihan, who also created the JEB Stuart statue along Richmond's Monument Avenue as well as two monuments at the Chickamauga and Chattanooga National Military Park.

The Stedman monument stands near the corner of Campfield Avenue and Bond Street, next to St. Augustine Church. A marker in the field honors Matthew Arace, a Hartford police officer killed in a 2006 automobile accident.

Across Campfield Avenue, a bronze plaque mounted on a granite slab honors Thomas McManus, a Hartford native and Civil War veteran who served as a major in the 25th Regiment. He was also a judge, a member of Connecticut's General Assembly and director of the state prison at Wethersfield.

USS Hartford Bell, Hartford

The bell of the famed warship USS *Hartford* is displayed in the city's Constitution Plaza.

The USS *Hartford*, launched in 1858 at the Boston Navy Yard, served as Admiral David Farragut's flagship during the Civil War. The *Hartford* was used to blockade Confederate ports, and was used during the capture of New Orleans in 1862, the Vicksburg siege in 1863, and the Battle of Mobile Bay in 1864.

The *Hartford's* bell sits in a pedestrian garden, just north of the Kinsley Street bridge and south of the granite clock tower (in front of the former Clarion Hotel).

A plaque at the base of its granite mounting reads, "Bell of the USS *Hartford*. Admiral Farragut's flagship during the Civil War Battles of New Orleans, April 1862, and Mobile Bay, August 1864. 'Damn the torpedoes…full speed ahead.' (Farragut at Mobile Bay.)"

After the Civil War, the *Hartford* served in the Pacific and later as a training ship until it was decommissioned in 1926. The ship was stored at Charleston for a dozen years before being transferred to Norfolk for restoration. The ship was allowed to deteriorate and eventually sank at its berth in 1956.

The *Hartford's* bell was rung in 1957 at the first convocation of students and faculty at the University of Hartford (where one of the ship's anchors is displayed).

The *Hartford's* figurehead is displayed in the lobby of the state capitol building. Other *Hartford* relics are displayed at the U.S. Navy Museum in Washington, the National Civil War Naval Museum, Mystic Seaport, Trinity College in Hartford, and other locations.

Civil War Monument, West Hartford

West Hartford honors its Civil War veterans with a simple memorial in the town's North Cemetery.

The Civil War monument, near the cemetery's central driveway, resembles a large-scale version of the traditional Union veteran headstone shape. (In contrast to the rounded top seen on Union headstones, Confederate stones usually have a pointed top.)

The West Hartford monument bears a dedication on its west face reading, "Erected 1904 by the State of Connecticut in memory of the men of West Hartford who offered up their lives, a sacrifice in the Civil War, 1861-1865, and whose bodies were never brought home for burial."

Under the dedication, the monument lists the names, regimental affiliations, and dates and places of death for 10 West Hartford residents lost in the war.

The monument's east face lists an additional name, as well as an excerpt from the Bivouac of the Dead poem seen in several national cemeteries and war memorials.

The monument was supplied by the Stephen Maslen Company, which also created Civil War monuments in Suffield and Canton.

Veterans Memorial, Avon

A red granite memorial with several panels honors Avon's war heroes and veterans.

The central panel of the monument, at the intersection of West Main Street (Routes 44 and 202) and Ensign Drive, honors Avon residents who died during service in the country's wars. The panel lists one veteran who died during the Mexican War; 25 during the Civil War; 13 from World War II; and two from Vietnam.

The memorial's other six panels list veterans of the wars between the Mexican War and the first Persian Gulf War in the early 1990s.

The monument also features a granite podium inscribed with

"Dedicated to veterans of all wars," the name of the local VFW post, and the monument's dedication dates in 1986 and 1996.

Soldiers' Monument, Weatogue

Simsbury honors its Civil War veterans with an 1895 monument in the Weatogue section of town.

The Soldiers' Monument features an infantryman standing with a rifle atop a rough granite pedestal. A dedication on the front (northeast) face reads, "Erected to the memory of Union soldiers in the War of the Rebellion 1861-1865." A GAR emblem also appears on the northeast face.

The monument's northwest and southwest sides bear large panels inscribed with the names of local Civil War veterans. The southeast side is inscribed with the names of 15 officers.

The monument was supplied by the Munson Granite Company, and the sculptor's name isn't readily available.

At the base of the monument, a dedication plaque was added in 1995 as part of the monument's 100th anniversary. The plaque dedicates the monument to all veterans of the Civil War, and lists 37 Simsbury residents who were lost in the conflict.

The monument stands in a small wooded area on Hopmeadow Street (Route 10), just south of the intersection with Sand Hill Road.

Memorial Gateway, Simsbury

The Memorial Gateway at the entrance of Simsbury Cemetery on Hopmeadow Street (Route 10), dedicated in 1923, honors residents killed in the Civil War and World War I. The gateway features two curved fences as well as pillars topped with bronze eagles.

Plaques are mounted within the brick gateway to honor local war heroes. The south plaque, which honors Civil War veterans, bears a dedication reading, "Erected to the memory and honor of those citizens of Simsbury who, by sacrifice and service during the Civil War, helped to maintain the integrity of the Union 1861-1865."

The north plaque bears a similar dedication to residents who served in World War I.

A large marker just inside the cemetery ground marks the location of the first meeting house in Simsbury, which was erected in 1683 and stood until 1739.

Nearby Monuments

Across the street from the cemetery, a monument outside Eno Memorial Hall honors local war veterans. A dedication on the monument's south side reads, "In memory of those from Simsbury who gave their lives in the service of their country. These dead shall not have died in vain."

The monument lists five residents who were killed in World War I, 17 who died in World War II, two who died in Korea, and three who were lost in Vietnam.

Canton Veterans' Memorial, Collinsville

Canton honors veterans of the Civil War and other conflicts with a 1903 monument in Village Cemetery.

The Veteran's Memorial, in the Collinsville section of Canton, honors veterans of the American Revolution, War of 1812, Civil War and Spanish-American War, and lists Civil War heroes whose bodies were not returned.

A dedication on the monument's south face reads, "Erected 1903 by the State of Connecticut and the Collinsville Cemetery Association in memory of the men of Canton who offered up their lives [as] a sacrifice in the Civil War, 1861-1865, and whose bodies were never brought home."

The south face also features an elaborate Connecticut state seal.

The north face features a bronze plaque listing 39 Canton residents who died during their Civil War service. Along with their names, the plaque lists their regimental affiliation, and the date and place of death.

The monument was supplied by the Stephen Maslen Corp., a Hartford granite dealer whose other Connecticut projects included the Soldiers' Monument in Suffield.

A flagpole stands near the monument, which is surrounded by smaller flags and flanked by shrubbery.

War Memorials, Burlington

Burlington honors its war veterans and heroes with several monuments on the green at the intersection of Spielman Highway (Route 4) and George Washington Turnpike.

At the western end of the green, a memorial honors Burlington's Civil War and World War I veterans. On the western side of the monument, a bronze plaque includes a dedication reading, "The Town of Burlington has not forgotten her beloved brothers who offered their lives to preserve the Union, 1861-1865."

Beneath the dedication are 88 names of Burlington residents or natives who served in the Civil War, with stars indicating the 20 residents who died during their Civil War service. The Civil War plaque was dedicated in 1998.

Among the veterans listed is Elijah W. Bacon, a private in the 14th Connecticut Volunteer Infantry who was awarded the Congressional Medal of Honor after the Battle of Gettysburg for capturing the 16th North Carolina's battle flag. Bacon was killed during the 1864 Battle of the Wilderness in Virginia.

On the east face of the monument, Burlington honors its World War I veterans. The monument's plaque includes a dedication reading, "Let us hold in honored memory those who served their country in the World War, 1917-1919."

The World War I monument includes 42 names, and highlights five residents who died during their service.

To the east of the Civil War and World War I memorial, an undated monument honors Burlington residents who served in World War II, Korea and Vietnam.

The western face of the monument bears an engraved eagle and an inscription reading, "Dedicated to the veterans of Burlington who served in the armed forces and died for our freedom."

Beneath this dedication, a tablet lists 118 names of residents who served in Vietnam, and honors two residents who were killed.

The east face of the monument has the same dedication as the west side, and bears two plaques honoring Burlington's World War II and Korea veterans. The World War II sections list 135 names, and honor seven residents who were killed. The Korea section lists 43 names.

Soldiers' Monument, Unionville

The Soldiers' Monument in the Unionville section of Farmington was dedicated in 1916 to honor local residents who served in the Civil War.

The monument features three figures. A standard-bearer stands atop the column, while its base is flanked by an artillery soldier on one side and an infantryman on the other. Infantry, artillery, cavalry and naval symbols grace the column. The front column also features the logo of the Grand Army of the Republic.

The front of the base is inscribed with a dedication reading, "Unionville honors the earth that wraps her heroes' clay."

The monument was funded primarily by Captain Nathaniel C. Hayden, a veteran of the 16th Regiment Connecticut Volunteers who was wounded in the battle of Antietam. Capt. Hayden was a successful local businessman who lobbied for funds to build the monument. Eventually, he had it built himself. Fortunately, he lived long enough to attend the dedication.

The monument, supplied by the McGovern Granite Co. of Hartford, sits near the First Church of Christ Congregational at the intersections of Main Street (Route 4), School Street and Lovely Street (Route 177).

Diagonally across the intersection is a memorial to 19 Unionville residents who died in the two World Wars, Korea and Vietnam.

Soldiers' Monument, Farmington

Farmington honors its Civil War heroes with a brownstone obelisk in Riverside Cemetery.

The Soldiers' Monument, erected in 1872, bears a dedication on its front (south) face reading, "To the memory of volunteer soldiers from this village."

The south face also bears the names of five residents killed in the war, and a decorative trophy featuring crossed rifles. The south face also honors the battle of Gettysburg, and the base includes the inscription, "They gave their lives for our country and freedom."

The east face includes five names, and honors the battle of Antietam. The base includes an inscribed poem reading, "How sleep the brave who sink to rest, by all their country's wishes blest."

The north face lists five names, as does the west face. The west face also honors the battle of Fort Wagner (S.C.), and features a raised United States seal. The west base bears the inscription, "God, preserve the nation in peace."

Information about the monument's designer or supplier has not come to light. The lettering has faded in several places, making it difficult to read, and the monument has large areas of lichen growth.

Directly across from the Soldiers' Monument, a memorial honors Farmington residents killed in the World Wars, Korea and Vietnam. The undated memorial lists two residents killed in World War I, nine in World War II, one in Korea and two in Vietnam.

A short walk west of the war memorials is the grave of Foone, one of the former Amistad slaves. Foone's grave is listed as a stop on the Connecticut Freedom Trail. A bronze plaque was placed in front of the grave in 2001 because the inscription was difficult to read.

Veterans' Memorial, Farmington

The Farmington Veterans' Memorial provides a comprehensive tribute to local residents who participated in wars and skirmishes.

The 1992 monument, in front of Town Hall and near the intersection of Farmington Avenue (Route 4) and Monteith Drive, features five granite columns inscribed with the names of residents who died while serving the nation.

The monument's front (northwest) face bears a simple inscription reading, "Duty, Honor, Country," and displays the five service branch emblems.

The monument's columns also list military conflicts starting with early battles not commonly listed on memorials, such as the English settlers' fights with the Pequots in the 1630s, the French and Indian Wars and the 1712 Defense of Litchfield.

More recent conflicts listed on the monuments include peacekeeping in Lebanon (1982-4), the Grenada invasion in 1983 and Operation Desert Storm in 1990-91.

Looking at major conflicts more typically cited on municipal war memorials, the Farmington monument lists the names of 11 residents killed or wounded in the American Revolution; 63 in the Civil War; eight in World War I; 18 in World War II; and five in the Vietnam war.

The monument's southeast face repeats the service emblems, but is otherwise unlettered.

A tree in front of the Veterans' Memorial is a descendent of Hartford's Charter Oak.

Soldiers' Monument, New Britain

New Britain honors its Civil War veterans with an elaborate monument in the heart of downtown.

The domed monument, at the north end of the city's Central Park, features a gilded allegorical figure representing Victory as well as gilded torches and a variety of classical architectural decorative elements including columns and seashells.

Inscriptions on the front (south) face include, "With malice toward none, with charity for all, with firmness in the right" from the conclusion of Lincoln's second Inaugural address, and, "Oh rare and royal was the sacrifice."

Inscriptions on the east face include the "Let us have peace," quote from U.S. Grant as well as a dedication reading, "This monument is built in grateful remembrance of the soldiers and sailors who in the war to maintain the Union offered their lives in the cause of mankind that coming generations, taught by their example, may cherish the fruits of their valor and devotion, and make their memory immortal."

The north face bears a quote from U.S. Sen. Daniel Webster, "Liberty and Union, now and forever, one inseparable."

An inscription on the west face lists the years of the Civil War in Roman numerals, as well as "Erected by the Citizens of New Britain 1899" (also in Roman numerals).

The east and west faces are also decorated with U.S. shields with eagles and crossed swords, and well as large lion heads above fountains that were later converted into planters.

Four pillars around the base bear the names of Civil War battles, and the monument's interior is inscribed with the names of local residents who fought in the war.

The allegorical Winged Victory figure holds an olive branch to symbolize the reconciliation of the Union and Confederate states. The figure was replaced in 2000 as part of a restoration performed for the monument's 100th anniversary.

The monument's architect, Ernest Flagg, was also responsible for the Singer Building and St. Luke's Hospital in New York, buildings for the U.S. Naval Academy, and several buildings in Hartford.

At the south end of the park, three monuments honor New Britain's veterans from World War II, Korea and Vietnam.

The Returned Soldier, Rocky Hill

An 1867 marble statue depicting a Civil War cavalry officer being greeted by a young girl stands outside Connecticut's home for veterans in Rocky Hill.

The statue was originally located in Darien at the state's first veterans' facility, Fitch's Home for Soldiers and Orphans. That facility was founded by Benjamin Fitch, a wealthy dry goods merchant, who helped raise a regiment and promised its members he would care for wounded veterans and their orphaned children.

Fitch's home became a state facility, and the population ebbed and flowed between the Civil War and the World War I before peaking at more than 1,000 soldiers during the Great Depression.

Recognizing the need for a bigger facility, the state opened the Rocky Hill home for veterans. The vets who moved to Rocky Hill included a 97-year-old Civil War veteran.

In 1950, the Returned Soldier statue was moved from the former Fitch Home site to Spring Grove Cemetery. More than 2,100 vets are buried at Spring Grove, the first veterans' cemetery in the state.

In 1985, the statue was moved to Rocky Hill, restored and placed on its granite base.

The statue was sculpted by Larkin Goldsmith Mead, a New Hampshire native who moved to Italy. Some of his other public works include the statues on Abraham Lincoln's tomb in Springfield, Illinois.

Soldiers' Monument, Berlin

An 1871 brownstone obelisk in East Berlin honors the service of local Civil War veterans.

The understated monument stands in a traffic island at the T-shaped intersection of Main and Berlin streets. An inscription at the base of the front (south) face reads "Soldiers." The south face also lists the names and unit affiliations of 14 veterans as well as the battles of Antietam and Gettysburg, and is also decorated with a Connecticut seal.

The east face lists nine names and the battles of Petersburg (Virginia) and Port Hudson (Louisiana). The north face lists the Confederate prison camps in Florence, South Carolina and Andersonville, Georgia, as well as 14 names. The west face lists 15 names and the battles of the Wilderness and Fredericksburg, both in Virginia.

The shaft is topped by funerary decorative elements, but otherwise is fairly plain. Obelisks were customary for Civil War monuments built in the 1860s and early 1870s.

The Berlin monument was erected by the local Grand Army of the Republic post. Overall, it remains in good condition, and only has a small amount of lichen growth.

Soldiers' Monument, Kensington

A brownstone obelisk in the Kensington section of Berlin is the oldest permanent Civil War monument in the United States.

The monument was dedicated July 28, 1863--less than a month

after the Battle of Gettysburg and 20 months before Lee's army surrendered at Appomattox Court House, Virginia.

The front (northeast) face of the monument bears the dedication, "Erected to commemorate the death of those who perished in suppressing the Southern rebellion," as well as a poem, "How sleep the brave who sink to rest, by all their country's wishes blest" and the year 1863.

The word "Soldiers" appears in large inscribed letters at the monument's base. The obelisk also features a Connecticut seal.

The northwest and southeast faces of the monument both bear the names, and the location and date of death, of four residents. The southwest face bears the same information for eight residents killed in the conflict. The names were added after the war ended.

The monument, at the intersection of Percival Avenue (Rte. 71) and Sheldon Street, was designed by Kensington resident Nelson Augustus Moore, a noted landscape artist and photographer.

The monument is surrounded by an ornate fence, to which several plaques have been affixed. One plaque lays claim to the Kensington obelisk being the "First monument in the United States dedicated to the soldiers of the Civil War – erected 1863". Another plaque was added on Memorial Day of 1961 by a local political party to commemorate the 100th anniversary of the start of the Civil War, and another plaque was attached when the monument was rededicated in July 2013 to honor its 150th anniversary.

The monument stands on the grounds of the Kensington Congregational Church, which formed in 1712. The parish's meetinghouse was built in 1774.

A cannon was added to the site in 1913 as part of 50th anniversary commemoration ceremonies.

War Memorials, Berlin

Berlin honors local war veterans with a collection of memorials on Worthington Ridge.

The monument site is dominated by a 1920 obelisk topped by a large eagle. A dedication on the east side of the obelisk's base reads, "Erected by the town of Berlin in honor of her patriotic men and women who served their country in time of war. For the dead, a tribute. For the living, a memory. For posterity, an emblem of loyalty to the flag of their country."

The other three sides of the monument have simple plaques listing a war and the dates in which it was fought. The north side honors World War I, the west side honors the Spanish-American War and the south side honors the Civil War.

Behind the obelisk is a curved brick pergola that features four monuments honoring veterans of the two World Wars, Korea and Vietnam.

World War I veterans are honored with a two-sided memorial at the south end of the pergola. Both sides bear two columns of names listing residents who served in the war. The west face of the World

War monument honors five residents killed in the conflict, including one who died in Red Cross service.

World War II veterans are honored with a similar two-sided tablet, each with four columns of names. The east face bears a dedication and honors 22 veterans killed in the conflict.

Veterans of the Korean and Vietnam wars are honored with single-sided tablets. The Korean War memorial has two columns of residents listed, and honors one resident killed in action. The Vietnam memorial, which has four columns of names, honors three residents killed in action and one who was reported missing.

A cannon facing west has been mounted in the central section of the pergola, between the World War II and Korean War memorials.

A marker installed in front of the obelisk honors 21 residents who served in Operation Desert Storm in 1991. Granite planters in the front of the monument site honor the branches of the military.

The monument stands in a park at the intersection where Farmington Avenue and Wildem Road meet Worthington Ridge.

Soldiers' Monument, Bristol

Bristol honors its Civil War veterans with an 1866 brownstone obelisk that's one of the state's earliest monuments commemorating the conflict.

The monument is a tall obelisk topped by a brownstone eagle. A dedication on the monument's front (east) side reads, "Erected by voluntary contributions in grateful remembrance of the volunteer soldiers of Bristol who gave up their lives in behalf of their country in the war of the great rebellion. The sacrifice was not in vain."

The east face also lists 14 Bristol residents killed in the Civil War. The east face also features the seals of Connecticut and the United States, and a decorative trophy depicting a flag, a rifle, a sword and a cartridge pouch. The east face also honors the battle of Antietam and men who died at the Confederate prisoner of war camp in Andersonville, Georgia.

The monument's north face lists 13 residents who died as prisoners of war, and two who were lost at sea. The battles of Fredericksburg (Virginia) and Plymouth (N.C.) are also listed.

The west face lists 13 names, and the battles of Fort Wagner (South Carolina) and Irish Bend (Louisiana.). The south face lists 12 names, and the battles of Gettysburg and New Bern (N.C.).

The monument was supplied by Hartford entrepreneur James Batterson, whose firm was responsible for a number of Civil War monuments in Connecticut and other locations.

Overall, the Bristol monument is good condition considering its age. The lettering on the base of the monument's east face is somewhat weathered and difficult to read, and cracks on the south face appear to have been patched with a material similar to auto-repair putty. Two braces have been affixed to the top of the column, just below the brownstone eagle.

The monument, on a hilltop in the city's West Cemetery, was dedicated in January of 1866, making it perhaps the second Civil War monument in Connecticut.

A low brownstone marker in front of the monument is dedicated "To the Unknown Dead," and a marker honoring all veterans has been placed to the west of the monument.

A number of Civil War veterans are buried in the section just east of the Soldiers' Monument.

In 2011, an additional monument honoring Bristol's Civil War veterans was dedicated on Memorial Boulevard.

Civil War Monument, Bristol

In 2011, Bristol erected a second monument to the memory of its Civil War veterans. The monument, on the city's Memorial Boulevard, was erected because the 54 names on the city's 1866 Civil War Monument, in West Cemetery, have become difficult to read.

The pink granite monument, next to the city's memorial to its World War II and Korea heroes, features a large engraved eagle and crossed cannons. A bronze plaque on the monument's north face reads, "Bristol's original Civil War monument was dedicated on January 20, 1866, and stands in the West Cemetery. The ravages of time are slowly destroying the soldier's names that appear on its weathered brownstone. To insure they are not forgotten, this new monument is dedicated to their memory. In memory of the men from Bristol who gave up their lives to preserve the Union."

The plaque also lists the 54 Bristol residents lost in the Civil War, and describes the history of the West Cemetery memorial.

The base of the monument honors the battles of Fredericksburg, Antietam and Plymouth.

Defenders of the Flag Monument, Plainville

Plainville honors local veterans with several monuments in a downtown park established in 1945.

Plainville's Civil War veterans are honored with the Defenders of the Flag Monument, which was dedicated in 1913. The granite monument features a standard-bearer and an inscription on its front (northwest) face with the simple dedication, "In memory of the defenders of the flag."

The monument's northwest face also features a large Grand Army of the Republic medallion just below the standard-bearer's feet, as well as crossed swords (representing the cavalry) and rifles (representing the infantry) above the years during which the Civil War was fought.

The standard-bear's pose is somewhat uncommon in that, unlike most Civil War monuments depicting a standard-bearer, the Plainville figure holds the flag with both hands. Most earlier standard-bearer monuments include a figure prepared to withdraw a sword to defend the colors.

The metal GAR marker near the base of the monument is unusually large and the first we've seen that has been painted. The cannon behind the monument was cast in 1863.

The monument, originally located on land that later became the site of Town Hall, replaced a wooden memorial in a local cemetery honoring the town's Civil War veterans.

The monument was supplied by the McGovern Granite Company of Hartford, whose other monuments in Connecticut include war memorials dedicated in Unionville, Old Saybrook, Stafford Springs and Newtown.

Along the Maple Street side of Veterans' Memorial Park, at the corner of Whiting and Maple street, a 1984 monument honors veterans of Korea and Vietnam. The granite monument, topped with an engraved eagle, features a dedication on its north face reading, "In honor of the men and women of this community who served in Korea and Vietnam."

Next to that monument, a 1991 monument honors Plainville residents who served in Operation Desert Storm.

Near the park's northwest corner, a stone monument with a large plaque honors Plainville's World War veterans. A dedication reads, "In honor of the men and women of Plainville who served in the Armed Forces during World War I & II. To the eternal memory of those who gave the last full measure of devotion and sacrifice."

The list of World War I dead contains nine names, and the section honoring World War II dead lists 31 residents.

Soldiers' Monument, Southington

Southington's Civil War veterans are honored with an 1880 monument in the center of the town green.

The granite Soldiers' Monument depicts a clean-shaven Civil War soldier standing with a rifle. A relatively simple dedication on the front (east) face reads, "The defenders of our Union. 1861-1865."

The east face also features an intricate carving of the Connecticut and United States shields and a raised ribbon with the state motto. The monument's other faces do not bear inscriptions.

While the monument has comparatively little lettering, it has a number of decorative elements not commonly seen on Civil War monuments, such as the four blue granite columns at each corner and the ornamental gables just below the soldier's feet.

The monument was created by Charles Conrads, the principal sculptor for James Batterson's New England Granite Works. Batterson supplied many Civil War monuments in Connecticut.

Nearby Monuments

North of the green, which was laid out in 1876, a memorial flagpole dedicated after World War I honors veterans of that conflict and the nation's earlier wars. On the east and north faces of the flagpole's base, bronze tablets list veterans of World War I (in four columns on each tablet).

On the west side, a tablet has four columns listing Southington's Civil War veterans. On the south side, veterans of the American Revolution, the War of 1812, the Mexican War, and the Spanish-American War are honored.

South of the Civil War monument, a collection of memorials honors veterans of World War II, Korea, Vietnam and the ongoing fight against terrorism. The central granite tablet bears a dedication inscribed below a carved eagle. The left two memorials feature bronze tablets listing World War II veterans in 10 long columns of names, and honoring 33 residents who were killed in the conflict.

The two memorials on the right honor veterans of World War II, Korea and Vietnam. The Korean War memorial list veterans in six columns and honors one who was killed. The Vietnam memorial also has six columns of names and honors 10 who were killed.

LITCHFIELD COUNTY

War Memorials, New Milford

New Milford honors local veterans and war heroes with a collection of monuments along the town green.

Just above the northern end of the green, a monument features a bronze bust of Abraham Lincoln. The front (south) side of the monument's base features an elongated oval plaque (not unlike a pressed penny) inscribed with the Gettysburg Address. The north side features a similar plaque explaining that the monument is a 1912 gift of Edward Williams Marsh, who served during the war in the Second Regiment, Connecticut Volunteers Heavy Artillery.

The monument is dedicated, "In loving memory of the soldiers and sailors of the Union Army and Navy, 1861-1865, and of Abraham Lincoln, President of the United States,1861-1865. Besides being in many skirmishes, the New Milford troops were engaged in the battles of Gettysburg, Cold Harbor (Va.), Petersburg (Va.),

Opequan (Va.), Fisher's Hill (Va.), Cedar Creek (Va.), Sailors Creek (Va)., Fort Fisher (N.C.)."

At the southern end of the New Milford green, a large monument honors local veterans. The monument features a large carved eagle, and an inscription on its southern face reads, "In recognition of service rendered to our country by [the] men and women of New Milford, Connecticut, during national crises." Below the inscription are the shields of the five military branches.

Just north of this monument is a restored World War II tank that, according to the New Milford Historical Society, was placed on the green in 1948 by the local VFW post.

To the east of these memorials, a flagpole honors New Milford's World War II veterans. A plaque on the flagpole's stone base lists 18 residents who lost their lives.

Continuing north, we find a granite monument that honors World War I veterans on its southern face and Civil War veterans on its northern side. The World War I plaque bears the dedication, "This tablet is dedicated in commemoration of the men of New Milford who served their country in the World War." Below the dedication are three columns of names, including 12 who were killed.

The Civil War plaque on the monument's northern face bears a nearly identical inscription that also appears above three columns of names. Two granite eagles flank the east and west sides of the monument's base.

Soldiers' Monument, New Preston

An undated monument in New Preston Village Cemetery honors local Civil War veterans.

The monument stands near the Baldwin Hill Road entrance to the cemetery, which is in the New Preston section of Washington.

A dedication on the monument's east face reads, "A memorial to the soldiers who served faithfully and honorably in the Civil War, 1861-1865. Erected by a comrade, Major Walter Burnham."

A small cannon has been mounted near the monument's base.

The monument's west face lists 23 Civil War veterans buried in the cemetery.

Information about the monument's designer or supplier hasn't come to light.

Walter Burnham, a local carriage and wagon manufacturer, sponsored the monument. Burnham served in the Second Connecticut Heavy Artillery regiment, and was wounded during the 1864 Battle of Cedar Creek (in Virginia's Shenandoah Valley.)

Soldiers' Monument, Kent

Kent honors its Civil War veterans with a granite 1885 obelisk in the intersection of North Main Street (Route 7) and Bridge Street (Route 341).

The simple obelisk stands slightly off-center in the middle of

Route 7, protected from traffic by four planters and a low curb.

A dedication on the monument's front (north) face reads, "A tribute of honor and gratitude to her citizens who fought for liberty and Union, 1861-1865". The bottom of the base is inscribed with the words, "Erected by the people of Kent, 1885."

The Connecticut shield is also engraved in the monument's north face. The monument's other faces are free of ornamentation.

The obelisk was originally closer to the center of the intersection, but was shifted west during a 1924 widening of Route 7.

Information about the monument's designer has not come to light, but the Kent obelisk has been attributed to architect Robert W. Hill, who designed the nearly identical 1871 Soldiers' Monument in Woodbury.

Soldiers' Monument, Sharon

The 1885 Soldiers' Monument at the northwest corner of Sharon's town green is the only Civil War monument in Connecticut topped with a granite cannon.

The distinctive monument was also among the first of the state's monuments to feature a curved bench at its base (the 24th Regiment monument in Middletown has a similar bench).

The front (east) face of the monument bears the dedication, "Erected by the town of Sharon in memory of the brave men who enlisted from this township in the War of the Rebellion and fell in the struggle to maintain the Union."

The monument's north, west and south faces list a total of 28 residents lost in the conflict.

According to a Sharon Historical Society newsletter, the cannon was damaged in the mid-20th century by local youths climbing on the monument. The granite cannon was then replaced by a wooden replica, and was returned to the monument during a 1998 restoration.

The monument was designed by Emily O. Wheeler who, with her sisters, also designed the 1884 stone clock tower about four-tenths of a mile south at the intersection of Main Street (Route 41) and Cornwall Hollow Road (Route 4).

A modern-era war memorial, across the street from the clock tower, has 13 granite panels listing local residents who served and died in wars ranging from the American Revolution to Desert Storm.

Civil War Monument, Salisbury

An allegorical figure holds a United States shield high above Salisbury's green as part of the town's 1891 Civil War monument.

The figure stands atop a granite base featuring cannon muzzles protruding from each side in an arrangement unique to Connecticut's

Civil War monuments.

The inclusion of cannons in the original design of the monument (for many monuments, government surplus cannons were added after the monument was dedicated) honors not only the service of local residents, but also Salisbury's importance as a source of high-quality iron used to cast artillery pieces during the war.

The front (south) face of the monument features a bronze state seal and the dedication, "To her loyal sons who fought for the Union, Salisbury erects this memorial 1891." The south face also lists the battles of Cold Harbor (Va.) and Olustee (Va.)

The east face has a plaque listing four columns of infantry and artillery soldiers, and honors the battles of Port Hudson (La.) and Winchester (Va.) The north face lists infantry soldiers and the battles of Gettysburg and Drewry's Bluff (Va.). The west face lists infantry soldiers, and the battles of Antietam and Petersburg (Va.)

Along with listing local soldiers who fought with a variety of Connecticut regiments, the monument's west face also honors Salisbury natives who fought with infantry, cavalry and artillery units in Illinois, Rhode Island, New York, Massachusetts, Ohio and the regular U.S. Army.

The figure atop the monument faces south and holds a United States shield. Broken shackles and a chain are visible near the figure's left foot, similar to the base of the Statue of Liberty.

The Salisbury monument is known variously as the Columbia, Union and Freedom monument, depending on which source you consult. Rather than adding to the confusion, we decided to describe it simply as the "Civil War Monument".

The monument's sculptor, George Bissell, who was also responsible for designing Civil War monuments in Waterbury, Winchester and Colchester.

John Sedgwick Monument, Cornwall Hollow

Cornwall Hollow native Major General John Sedgwick, who was killed at the Battle of Spotsylvania Court House (Va.), is honored in his hometown with a monument at the intersection of Cornwall Hollow Road (Route 43) and Hautboy Hill Road.

The monument features a large granite slab that bears a bronze plaque depicting Sedgwick on the front (south) face. The dedication reads, "This memorial, including ordnance used in the Mexican and Civil Wars and given by the government of the United States, in honour of Major General John Sedgwick, Commander of the Sixth Corps, Army of the Potomac, who gave his life for the preservation of the Union."

Beneath this dedication, the monument bears an inscription reading: "A skilled soldier, a brave leader, a beloved commander and a loyal gentleman" and, "The fittest place where man can die is where man dies for man."

The north face lists some of Sedgwick's battles in the Mexican-American War (Vera Cruz, Cerra Gordo, Puerla, Cherribusco, Molino Del Ray) and the Civil War (Fair Oaks, Antietam, Fredericksburg, the

Wilderness and Spotsylvania).

An 1839 cannon stands on a granite base with a bronze eagle on its south face and wreaths on the east and west faces. The monument's base has six pyramids of concrete cannonballs. The monument's original cannonballs were removed in a World War II scrap drive (a common fate for cannonballs and artillery pieces used in Civil War monuments).

The Sedgwick monument was originally dedicated in 1900. The monument was vandalized in 1976 and the 1980s, and most of the bronze ornamentation was stolen. Replicas were cast, based on photos of the originals, and the monument was rededicated in 1994.

Sedgwick, born in 1830, graduated from West Point in 1837 and served in the artillery during the Mexican-American War. During the Civil War, he commanded the Sixth Corps of the Army of the Potomac.

Sedgwick was killed by a Confederate sniper on May 9, 1864, while directing artillery placement at Spotsylvania Court House. Sedgwick, attempting to rally his troops, said snipers (about 1,000 yards from Union troops) "couldn't hit an elephant at this distance" just before being shot below his left eye.

Sedgwick is buried in the Cornwall Hollow Cemetery on the other side of the road. His grave, a tall obelisk, features the Sixth Corps emblem and the dates and location of his birth and death.

A small marker immediately north of the Sedgwick monument indicates local schoolchildren planted a tree at the site in 1950. That tree has been removed, but a replacement has been planted.

Sedgwick is also honored with statues at Gettysburg and West Point (often touched by students for luck) as well as a monument at the Spotsylvania battlefield.

Soldiers' Monument, Norfolk

Veterans of the Civil War and later conflicts are honored with monuments on the green in Norfolk.

The 1868 Soldiers' Monument, one of the earliest tributes to Civil War veterans in Connecticut, is a tall granite obelisk similar to monuments in Plymouth, North Branford and other monuments dedicated in the 1860s.

The Norfolk monument bears a dedication on its western face reading, "To the memory of the soldiers from this town who died for their country in the War of the Rebellion."

The western face also lists the names and dates of death of seven residents killed in the Civil War.

The southern, eastern and northern faces list each list nine or 10 names and dates of death, in rough alphabetical order.

The monument was supplied by William Burdick, an agent of the Westerly, Rhode Island, granite quarries who also prepared the North Branford Civil War monument.

At the northern end of the green, an undated Honor Roll monument commemorates local veterans who died or served in more recent conflicts.

At the south end of the green, a memorial fountain dedicated in 1889 honors Joseph Battell, a local merchant whose family was long active in civil and philanthropic affairs.

The fountain, designed by noted architect Stanford White, features a central column supporting a sphere. Water emerges from three fish near the top of the column as well as a lion's head on its southern face.

The town's World War I veterans are honored with a monument at the intersection of Greenwoods Road (Route 44) and North Street (Route 272).

Winchester Soldiers' Monument, Winsted

Winchester honors its Civil War veterans with a magnificent 64-foot medieval tower on a hill overlooking the town.

The Winchester Soldiers' Monument, dedicated in 1890, is the largest feature in a Crown Street park in the Winsted section of

Winchester. The monument features a corner tower topped by an eight-foot bronze standard-bearer.

A granite archway in front of a long stairway that leads visitors to the monument tower bears the years of the Civil War.

A marker on the front (west) face of the monument reads, "Soldiers Memorial." Below the marker, a small plaque honors the monument's inclusion on the National Register of Historic Places.

The monument's three-story interior includes a dedication plaque reading, "Erected by the citizens of Winchester in recognition of their obligation to the loyal men who represented them during the War of the Rebellion, whose names are herein perpetuated in grateful remembrance of their patriotic service, 1861-1865."

The monument's interior includes granite markers listing the approximately 300 local residents who served in the war, as well as a fireplace.

A bronze door that depicted scenes from the war was lost to a World War II scrap drive. During the war, the monument was used as an observation tower. A wooden structure was added to the roof, and the site was electrified.

The park surrounding the monument also includes two cannons, a fountain/planter and a bulletin board describing the monument and its history.

The monument was designed by architect Robert W. Hill, who was also responsible for several state armories, opera houses in New Britain and Thomaston, the Litchfield county courthouse, and other public and private buildings.

The standard-bearer was created by George E. Bissell, whose other works included impressive Civil War monuments in Waterbury, Colchester and Salisbury.

The Winchester monument was been repaired several times in its history. Broken windows were replaced in the late 1970s. Since the early 1990s, a municipal commission has overseen the ongoing restoration of the monument.

A number of road signs helpfully direct visitors from downtown to the monument, which is open to the public during the afternoons of Memorial Day, Independence Day, Labor Day and Veteran's Day.

Soldiers' Monument, Winsted

The 1904 Soldiers' Monument in the Winsted section of Winchester stands at the south end of East End Park, near the green's intersection with Main Street (Route 44).

The 27-foot monument features an infantryman standing atop a large granite shaft. A dedication on the monument's front (south) face reads, "For the dead, a tribute. For the living, a memory. For posterity, an emblem of loyalty to the flag of their country."

The south face also features a decorative trophy with an eagle and two crossed flags, and honors the Battle of Cold Harbor.

The east face bears three crossed rifles, symbolizing the infantry, and honors the Battle of Antietam.

The north face has another dedication reading, "In honor of the patriotism and to perpetuate the memory of the 368 brave men who went forth from this town from 1861 to 1865 and periled their all that the nation might live, this monument has been erected so that all who come after them may be mindful of their deeds and fail not in the day of trial to emulate their example."

The north face also features the state seal and honors the Battle of

Port Hudson, La.

The west face displays crossed cannons, symbolizing the artillery, and honors the Battle of Petersburg, Va.

The monument was donated by Winsted native Charles Pine, who served in the Civil War and later became president of the Ansonia National Bank. Pine also donated a memorial chapel in Ansonia's Pine Grove Cemetery.

The monument was dedicated in May of 1905.

Moving slightly north on the green, a 2000 memorial to the 1,551 Winchester residents who served in World War II lists 39 names of residents killed in the conflict.

At the north end of the green, a granite pillar honors three residents killed in Vietnam.

To the west of the green, near the entrance to the Winsted Old Burying Ground cemetery, a 1907 monument honors the 44 American Revolution veterans buried within Winchester's borders.

At the south end of the green, a 1956 monument honors seven residents killed in the Naugatuck River Valley flood of 1955.

Forest View Cemetery, Winsted

Winchester honors veterans of the Civil War, World War I and other conflicts with several monuments in Forest View Cemetery.

The Non-Repatriated Soldiers' Monument, in the Winsted section of Winchester, was dedicated in 1900 to honor local Civil War heroes buried on distant battlefields.

The dark granite monument, topped with a polished sphere, stands at the center of a section of the cemetery with 21 graves of Civil War veterans who died after the war.

A dedication on the front (south) face of the monument reads, "Erected by the State of Connecticut and citizens of the town in memory of Winchester volunteers who died or were killed in the War of the Rebellion, and whose bodies were not brought home for burial."

The south face also bears the years of the Civil War, the United States seal and crossed flags, and the Latin inscription "Pro Patria" (for one's country).

The monument's east face lists the names and regimental affiliations of 21 residents lost in the conflict. The north face honors

10 residents whose service was credited to other towns, and the west face lists 22 residents.

According to the Connecticut Historical Society, information about the monument's designer or supplier isn't readily available.

The corners of the Civil War burial section have supports that once held round objects, such as cannonballs or granite spheres. Cannonballs incorporated into Civil War monuments have been removed in several other Connecticut locations, often due to theft, vandalism or World War II scrap metal drives.

To the immediate north of the Civil War section is the burial place of Samuel Belton Horne, a Winsted resident who received a Congressional Medal of Honor for actions in 1864.

At the western edge of Forest View Cemetery is a brownstone obelisk marking the grave of Col. Elisha S. Kellogg, a member of the 2nd Regiment of the Connecticut Volunteer Artillery who was killed in 1864 during the Battle of Cold Harbor, Va.

A number of graves near the Kellogg obelisk also list service in the Civil War.

Honoring Other Veterans

Near Forest View's entrance on Torrington Road, a 1923 monument and a grove honor Winchester's World War I veterans.

The monument features a bronze plaque mounted on a boulder surrounded by trees. The plaque has a dedication reading, "To keep in remembrance the men of Winchester who gave their service, even unto death, for their country and her kindred nations beyond the seas, 1917 – 1918, this tablet is erected and these oaks stand as a living memorial."

The plaque honors 16 residents lost in the First World War.

At the base of a hillside near the north end of the cemetery, two rows of graves honor veterans of more recent wars.

Soldiers' Monument, Barkhamsted

Barkhamsted honors its Civil War veterans with a granite obelisk that also commemorates the service of residents in later wars.

The Soldier's Monument, located near the intersection of Pleasant Valley Road (Route 318) and Beach Rock Road, was first dedicated in 1897 to honor veterans of the American Revolution, War of 1812, Mexican War and the Civil War.

In recent years, bronze plaques attached to the monument's base honor veterans of the Spanish-American War, the two World Wars, Korea and Vietnam.

A dedication on the monument's front (north) face reads, "The tribute of the people of Barkhamsted to the memory of her sons and daughters who fought to establish, defend and preserve the nation, erected 1897."

The north face also bears a decorative trophy with two crossed rifles in front of a wreath, and a plaque attached to the north base honors veterans of World War II and Korea.

The west face has a plaque honoring American Revolution veterans, and the base honors Korea and Vietnam veterans.

The south face commemorates residents who served in the Wars of 1812 and Mexico, and the base has a plaque (probably from 1939) listing names omitted from the 1897 plaques.

The east face honors veterans of the Civil War. The base honors Spanish-American War veterans as well as residents who served in World War I.

The monument was donated by Walter S. Carter, a Barkhamsted native who headed a New York law firm. In addition to the monument, Carter donated land and money to establish a cemetery in Barkhamsted.

The monument, like many of the graves in Center Cemetery to the south of the monument, was originally in the Barkhamsted Hollow section of town. The hollow was flooded in the 1930s when Saville Dam was built to create Barkhamsted Reservoir, which contributes to Hartford's water supply.

Two Barkhamsted cemeteries and the monument were relocated in 1939 and Center Cemetery was established. A section at the southern end of the cemetery honors residents whose remains could not be identified when they were moved.

To the east of the Soldiers' Monument, the bell from the former Hollow Church has been mounted on large granite blocks that originally formed part of the Saville Dam spillway.

Soldiers' and Sailors' Monument, New Hartford

New Hartford honors its Civil War veterans with a monument in the southwest corner of Village Cemetery.

The Soldiers' and Sailors' Monument stands near the cemetery entrance along Town Hill Road (Route 219).

A dedication on the monument's front (south) base reads, "Erected 1892 to the memory of New Hartford soldiers and sailors who served in the War of the Rebellion, 1861 1865."

The south face also displays a medallion representing the Grand Army of the Republic, the post-Civil War veterans' organization.

The east face bears a bronze plaque listing about 60 New Hartford residents or natives who served in the conflict. The north and west faces also have plaques honoring New Hartford's Civil War veterans.

The monument was supplied by the Temple Brothers of Rutland, Vermont. The New Hartford monument is believed to be the only Civil War memorial in Connecticut supplied by the firm.

A number of veterans of the Civil War and later conflicts are buried in the section to the immediate north of the monument.

Coe Memorial Park, Torrington

Several monuments honoring the wartime service of local residents grace Coe Memorial Park in downtown Torrington.

At the north end of the park, near the intersection of Main Street and Litchfield Turnpike (Route 202), stands the Wolcottville Soldiers'

Monument (which reflects the name of the city during the monument's dedication in 1879).

The monument, with a round shaft, features an infantry soldier holding a rifle. The front (north) face includes the Connecticut and U.S. shields above a dedication, "to the defenders of the Union."

The monument's south face lists the battles of Gettysburg and Antietam, as well as Virginia battles at Winchester, Malvern Hill, Cold Harbor, Petersburg and Cedar Creek.

The monument, supplied by James Batterson's New England Granite Works, was moved to the park from its former location in front of City Hall in 1936.

Nearby Monuments

Near the center of Coe Memorial Park is a large flagpole with a six-sided base that honors veterans from conflicts including the two World Wars, the American Revolution, the Spanish-American War, Korea, Vietnam, and the Civil War. A plaque also singles out local Italian American veterans for recognition.

Near the flagpole monument, the local VFW post donated an impressive 155-mm howitzer. At the southern end of the park, a stone fountain honors local Vietnam veterans and heroes.

Coe Memorial Park was donated to the city in 1908 by the children of Lyman Wetmore Coe and his wife, Eliza Seymour Coe. Mr. Coe was the owner of a local brass company, and the park was the site of their homestead.

John Brown Birthplace, Torrington

Abolitionist John Brown, hanged after an ill-fated raid on a Federal armory in Harpers Ferry, was born in 1800 on what is now John Brown Road in Torrington.

The site, listed on Connecticut's Freedom Trail, today consists of a small roadside clearing surrounded by a stone wall. A boulder, erected in 1932, has an inscription on its south side reading, "In a house on this site, John Brown was born May 9, 1800."

The site also has a wayside marker explaining the homestead was destroyed in a fire in 1918. Within the clearing, there are few signs of the former house, other than a large boulder at the eastern end of the property with a round hole that appears to have been part of a well or cistern.

The Brown family moved to Ohio in 1805. Brown moved to Massachusetts in 1816 before returning to Litchfield to study to become a minister. Eye inflammation and a lack of money prompted Brown to return to Ohio.

In 1856, Brown and his followers killed five pro-slavery Southerners, one of several violent incidents that year in Kansas as supporters and opponents fought over whether slavery would be allowed in the territory.

During the Harpers Ferry attack in 1859, Brown led followers who tried to seize the Federal armory in hopes of using the weapons to instigate a slave rebellion. Most of the attackers were killed or captured, and Brown was eventually surrounded in the armory's engine house. After a standoff, U.S. troops led by Robert E. Lee stormed the engine house and captured Brown, who was convicted of treason and hanged on December 2, 1859. He was buried in North Elba, N.Y.

Brown's raid, trial and execution helped further inflame the slavery debate that would lead to the Civil War.

Pro Patria Monument, Litchfield

Litchfield honors its Civil War heroes with a marble obelisk on the town green.

A dedication on the front (south) face of the monument, which was dedicated in 1874, reads, "Pro Patria" ("For one's country" in

Latin). The dedication is the centerpiece of an artistic bas relief featuring two weeping soldiers, draped flags, crossed rifles and cannonballs.

The south shaft also features an intricate Connecticut seal (a ribbon with the state motto extends beyond the shaft's edges), four flags and a cross to symbolize the Army of the Potomac's Sixth Corps. The south shaft also lists the battles of Fisher's Hill and Fort Darling, both in Virginia.

The east face contains the names, regimental affiliation, and the date and place of death of 20 residents lost in the conflict, and lists the battles of Antietam and Fort Harrison (Va.)

The north face honors 17 residents killed in the war, and lists the battles of Petersburg and North Anna, both in Virginia.

The west face lists 19 residents, as well as the battles of Winchester and Cold Harbor, both in Virginia.

Litchfield's choice of marble for its Civil War monument is uncommon in Connecticut, and it is likely that the marble was quarried nearby. The monument has held its details very well, considering its age and the relative softness of marble (compared with granite).

Additional information about the monument's sculptor or supplier is not readily available.

Mustered Out Monument, Litchfield

A monument in Litchfield's West Cemetery honors local Civil War heroes, including 23 buried on distant battlefields.

The monument, at the center of a cemetery section known as the Soldiers' Lot, features a granite drum and the simple inscription, "Mustered Out."

The monument was erected in 1894 as part of the dedication of a section of the cemetery for Civil War veterans. In 1903, the state of Connecticut erected 23 headstones to honor Civil War heroes who rest in unmarked battlefield graves.

Soldiers' Lot has a total of 35 headstones honoring Civil War veterans, as well as a stone honoring a local Marine sergeant who was killed in Vietnam in 1965.

Four large cannonballs mark the corners of the soldiers' section.

The cemetery is on Whites Woods Road in Litchfield.

Civil War Monument, Northfield

A brownstone obelisk erected in the village of Northfield in 1866 was one of the state's earliest Civil War monuments.

The monument stands on the village green in the Northfield section of Litchfield. The front (south) face bears the dedication, "That the generations to come might know them," "Lincoln" in raised letters, and the names of three local men who died in the war. Two were killed at the Battle of Winchester, Va., in 1864, and the other died at the Battle of Fishers Hill, Va., in 1864.

The east face of the monument lists two names – a hospital death at Alexandria, Va., in 1863 and a battle death from Cold Harbor, Va., in 1864. The north face records two deaths – one from the 1863 battle at Chancellorsville, Va., and another at Cold Harbor.

The west face records a death at the Battle of Antietam in 1862, as well as a death in an unspecified Virginia hospital in 1864.

A decorative urn, as well as a carved sculpture depicting an eternal flame, stands atop the monument's shaft.

The monument was carved by Nelson Bolles from the nearby Marble Dale section of New Preston.

Soldiers' Monument, Thomaston

Thomaston's Civil War monument, dedicated in 1902, stands in a small park surrounded by monuments to the two World Wars and more recent conflicts.

The Soldiers' Monument is a multi-layered, square granite shaft topped by a caped infantryman holding a rifle. The front (west) side of the shaft bears the dedication, "Erected by C.L. Russell Post, No. 68, G.A.R. and citizens, in commemoration of the soldiers who served in the Civil War." (The G.A.R. refers to the Grand Army of the Republic, the post-Civil War veterans organization.)

The west face also bears a symbolic eagle in front of two crossed flags, and the battle of Cold Harbor (Va.) is displayed just below the infantryman's feet.

The south face commemorates the battle of Gettysburg and features an ornate wreath. The east face honors the battle of Cedar Creek (Va.) and displays the seal of the state of Connecticut. The north face bears a GAR medal and commemorates the battle of Appomattox (Va.), the site of General Lee's surrender.

An 1863 cannon stands to the north of the monument, and a later-vintage cannon (perhaps from World War I) stands on the south side of the monument.

Nearby Monuments

Behind the Civil War monument, a memorial honors veterans from World War II, Korea, Vietnam and the Persian Gulf. Several bronze plaques list local residents who served in these conflicts, with the World War II monument listing an estimated 1,200 names among its five columns. The Korean conflict plaques list more than 165 names, and the Vietnam plaques list about 225 names.

The southwest corner of the park features the World War I Roll of Honor, which was dedicated "by the town of Thomaston to those who served their country in the World War."

The monument also features a stylized representation of Liberty standing between a soldier and a sailor, who are surrounded with symbolic flourishes including an airplane, a lighthouse, a cannon and other decorative elements.

Below these elements is a bronze plaque with four columns of names honoring members of the Army, Navy, Marines and 10 Red Cross and Army nurses.

Soldiers' Monument, Plymouth

One of the state's oldest Civil War monuments stands on the green in Plymouth.

Although the dedication date of the monument was not recorded, local tradition and its design indicate it was completed shortly after the Civil War ended in 1865.

The monument is a tasteful obelisk, similar to monuments in Northfield and North Branford that were dedicated in 1866. The front (south) face bears the dedication reading, "Erected to perpetuate the memory of those who lost their lives in the War of 1861" (this is an uncommon reference to the conflict, which is usually described as the "War to Preserve the Union" or the "War of the Rebellion").

As the Northfield obelisk does, the Plymouth monument also bears Lincoln's name on its front face.

The south face of the Plymouth monument also lists eight names, including one who is honored for his service as a chaplain. The east, north and west faces each list the names of 10 residents who served in the war.

The corners of the obelisk are framed with carved cannons.

Nearby Monuments

About 2.5 miles east of the green, Plymouth honors veterans of recent wars with three monuments in a Main Street park.

The Plymouth Veterans' Monument, near the intersection of Main Street (Route 6) and North Main Street, features a monument honoring the two World Wars and Korea, as well as a monument commemorating the Vietnam War.

A short walk northeast of the monument, a bronze plaque on a large boulder honors veterans of the two World Wars.

Soldiers' Monument, Terryville

An obelisk in Terryville's Hillside Cemetery honors the service of local residents killed in the Civil War.

The dedication date of the monument, in the Terryville section of Plymouth, was not recorded. But like its neighbor on the Plymouth green, its unadorned design indicates it was probably erected in 1865 or 1866.

Bronze tablets listing residents killed during the war were added in 1983 because the original inscriptions had faded.

The monument does not have a formal dedication message, other than the word "Soldiers" on its front (southwest) face. The bronze plaque above this dedication lists the names, ages and dates of death of six residents who were lost in the war.

The southeast and northeast face of the monuments both honor six local residents, and five residents are honored on the northwest face of the monument.

Looking at the ages of the Civil War heroes from Terryville reminds us of the relative youth of the soldiers involved in the conflict (as well as those serving the nation today). Of the 23 people listed on the monument, 11 died in their twenties, and six were killed in their teens. Three men were killed in their thirties, and three more in their forties.

A number of veterans from the Civil War and later conflicts are buried in the section surrounding the monument.

Soldiers' Monument, Watertown

Watertown honors the sacrifice of its Civil War veterans with a 1908 monument rising above DeForest Street (Route 6).

The monument features a round granite column topped by a bronze eagle. The front (southeast) face of the shaft is decorated with wreaths and flags rising above the dates of the Civil War.

The dedication, carved into granite, reads, "In commemoration of the patriotism and valor of the men of Watertown who, in the hour of peril, offered their lives that the republic might live, thus winning the gratitude of their fellow-citizens, the admiration of succeeding generations and a place among the nation's heroes; this monument is erected that their example may serve as an inspiration to heroic deeds in all coming time."

Three bronze plaques on the monument base bear about 104 names (some of which are now difficult to discern) and regimental affiliations. One of the units, the 29th, was comprised primarily of African-American volunteers, and the Watertown monument was one of the first in the state to highlight their service. (The unit is also honored with monuments in New Haven and Danbury.)

Atop the monument, a bronze eagle sits on a sphere. The column is also topped by decorative ornamentation, as well as United States shields on each of its four faces.

The monument was supplied by the Thomas Phillips & Son Company of New Haven.

Nearby Monuments

Across the street, the town dedicated a monument in 1921 to honor its World War I veterans. The boulder bears two bronze plaques, as well as a plaque commemorating the four local residents killed in Vietnam.

ABOUT THE AUTHOR

Dave Pelland is the editor of the Connecticut history blogs
ctmonuments.net and ctpostcards.net

25441340R00138

Made in the USA
Charleston, SC
30 December 2013